ANDREW JACKSON
Frontier President

Notable Americans

ANDREW JACKSON
Frontier President

Nancy Whitelaw

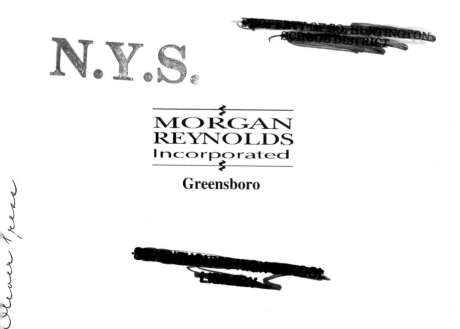

**MORGAN
REYNOLDS**
Incorporated

Greensboro

ANDREW JACKSON: FRONTIER PRESIDENT

Photo Credits: Courtesy of Library of Congress

Library of Congress Cataloging-in-Publication Data
Whitelaw, Nancy
    Andrew Jackson : frontier president / Nancy Whitelaw.-- 1st ed.
        p. cm. — (Notable Americans)
    Includes bibliographical references and (p.) and index.
    Summary: A biography of the seventh president from his childhood in South Carolina,
    through his military career in the War of 1812, to his death.
    ISBN 1-883846-67-6 (lib. bdg.)
        1. Jackson, Andrew, 1767-1845--Juvenile literature. 2. Presidents--United
States--Biography--Juvenile literature. [1. Jackson, Andrew, 1767-1845. 2. Presidents.] I.
Title. II. Series.

E382.W5.2000
973.5'6'092--dc21
[B]
                                                                    00-025559

Printed in the United States of America
First Edition

*Dedicated to Mary Jean Irion and Janette Martin—
with love and many thanks for all your work with the
Writer's Center at Chautauqua Institution.*

Có ....

Contents

Andrew Jackson

Chapter One

Sweet Retirement

Young Andrew Jackson's mother, Elizabeth, thought he should be a minister, but nobody else thought so. Not his classmates who said he was a bully. Not his friend who said that Andrew would fight at the drop of a hat; a hat Andrew most probably would drop himself. Not the neighbors who objected to his loud cursing and swearing. Everyone seemed to believe that Andrew's handsome face and bright blue eyes hid a mean and vicious temper. Still, Elizabeth hoped and prayed for her son.

There was not much money in the Jackson household. Andrew's father had died before Andrew was born, leaving Elizabeth with a four-year-old, a two-year-old, and an infant-to-come. After baby Andrew's birth on March 15, 1767, Elizabeth had to abandon the family farm and move in with her married sister Jane Crawford in Waxhaw, South Carolina.

Elizabeth chose to spend her meager income to send Andrew, not his older brothers, to a local Presbyterian academy. Andrew learned little or nothing about history, political science, grammar, literature, science, or higher math. He enjoyed writing. He did not care if he lacked the polish of the formal essayists who were popular then; he made up his own rules for spelling and punctuation. He enjoyed reading for his illiterate neighbors who gathered regularly in the local tavern to hear him read newspapers and public documents.

As he grew older, Andrew loved riding, racing, and caring for horses. He also enjoyed cockfighting, a popular sport in the South and West in the late eighteenth century. Historians have found a paper he wrote when he was about eleven years old. The paper began: "A Memorandum How to feed a Cock before you him fight Take and give him some Pickle Beaf Cut fine . . ."

Andrew was nine when the Declaration of Independence was signed. The Revolutionary War seemed far away from him. When British soldiers streamed into South Carolina in 1780, however, the war reached young Andrew firsthand. Some Americans were killed and 150 were wounded. Elizabeth worked in the makeshift hospital in Waxhaw, and Andrew helped her. There he heard tales of barbarism on the battlefields, tales that meant more to him than any history lesson he had sat through. Andrew's oldest brother, sixteen-year-old Hugh, was killed when his regiment was attacked. Andrew and his next oldest brother, Robert, took part in drills with the local soldiers. He developed a love of the military. Through contact with other soldiers, he began to understand that his country, the new United States of America, extended far beyond Waxhaw, South Carolina.

When Andrew was thirteen, he rode to war for the first time. No one is sure what his military assignments were. Probably he was a messenger boy between regiments, and perhaps he helped carry water or medicines to the troops. He learned to use his musket while riding horseback in shoot-hide-shoot guerilla warfare. He was captured by the British in 1781. A British officer ordered him to shine his boots. Andrew refused. The officer slashed at him with his sword. The blow left a large gash on

Thomas Jefferson (standing) drafted the Declaration of Independence based on the ideas of a congressional committee comprised of himself, Benjamin Franklin (left) and John Adams (center). The two remaining committee members (not pictured) were Roger Sherman and Robert R. Livingston.

Andrew's head which bled profusely but was not serious. As punishment, Andrew and his brother were both thrown into a prisoner of war camp. They received very little food and no medical attention, although smallpox was spreading around the camp. Most difficult for Andrew was the humiliation of taking orders.

Meanwhile, Elizabeth was nursing American troops. She soon found out her sons had been captured by the British. Somehow she was able to persuade the British to trade her two sons for two captive British soldiers. Robert died of smallpox shortly after his rescue. Andrew also became delirious from smallpox and nearly died. He later described his condition: "I was a skeleton—not quite six feet long and a little over six inches thick!" His mother nursed him back to health for several months.

Elizabeth volunteered next to help wounded soldiers in Charleston, South Carolina. For a few weeks after she left, Andrew heard nothing from her. Then he received a small bundle of her clothes. His mother had died of cholera, an infectious disease that spread quickly through the prison ships where she worked. Fifteen-year-old Andrew had lost his father, his two brothers, and now his mother.

He could not get along in the Crawford home so he was sent to live with another relative. There he worked in a saddler's shop and enjoyed the company of young men his age. As his depression lifted, he became more outgoing and was soon involved in drinking, gambling, and cockfighting.

In December 1782, Andrew moved to Charleston, taking with him 400 British pounds, an inheritance left by his Irish grandfather. In no time at all, he spent the inheritance and found himself in debt. To try to get back on his feet, Andrew played a round of craps.

It was a winner-take-all game, and Andrew put up his horse. The other players put up $200. Andrew won. He paid off his debts and rode his horse back to Waxhaw where he felt confident that he could become rich and famous. He took a few classes and set himself up as a teacher. Although barely a step ahead of his students, he earned enough money to live on. But Andrew wanted more money and more fame.

He decided to become a lawyer. He was accepted as a student by an attorney in Salisbury, North Carolina, who allowed him to work off some of his tuition. He enjoyed a social life with other students and was a leader, excelling in horse racing, cock fighting, card playing, dancing, and drinking. Some nights he drank heavily, and reports told of him smashing glasses, tearing up clothes and curtains, breaking up furniture, and even setting fire to a tavern. He earned a reputation as the heaviest student drinker in Salisbury.

Those who were not repelled by his rowdiness were attracted to Andrew's charm. He practiced grace and manners when he wished and was very charismatic. He had grown to six feet and one inch tall, was very thin with red hair and deep blue eyes, and had an energy that seemed ready to explode from his body.

In September 1787, he passed a bar examination before two judges to become a professional lawyer. He had learned only a little about the law but enough to allow him to practice temporarily. The only records of the next year show that he was arrested for trespassing and managed to settle the matter without fine or imprisonment.

In 1788, twenty-one-year old Andrew Jackson became the public prosecutor for a judge in the frontier area of what was then western North Carolina but would soon become the state of Tennessee. He hoped to enjoy life in this wilderness area, away from the rapidly growing cities where he had spent the last several years. The first community Jackson lived in was Jonesborough, a settlement of about sixty log cabins, 200 miles east of Nashville. After settling in, Jackson spent $300 to buy a nineteen-year-old slave named Nancy. He went often to the race track where he soon became known as both spectator and jockey. Jonesborough is probably the place where Jackson fought his first duel over an argument with another lawyer. In a fit of temper after a hearing, Jackson sent the defense attorney, Waightsill Avery, a challenge. His note said in part: "My character you have injured; and further you have Insulted me in the presence of a court and larg audianc I therefore call upon you as a gentleman to give me satisfaction."

Avery accepted the challenge. On the agreed-upon day, the men met just after sundown. They took their positions. The two men both fired at the same time into the air. Then they shook hands and walked away from the scene. They had proved that they were brave enough to accept a challenge and reasonable enough not to fire at each other.

A short time later Jackson moved to Nashville, Tennessee. In the 1780's, Nashville was a town of a few hundred people, a courthouse, two stores, and two taverns. The land was fertile, and the forests were rich in valuable hardwood. The promise of the land created major conflict between the Native Americans, who had lived there for generations, and the new settlers who wanted to profit from the land. The result of the conflict was increasing harassment on both sides.

Jackson moved into a boarding house with a family named Donelson. He found more than bed and board there. He also found seventeen-year-old Rachel Donelson Robards, a young wife known for her beautiful dark eyes and vivacious personality. Her husband Lewis Robards was away on frequent business trips. During Robard's absences, Jackson and Rachel, both fun-loving and impetuous, found much to talk about. Jackson's relationship with Rachel became the subject of town gossip, then, to some people, a scandal. The competition between Jackson and Robards grew. In December 1790, Robards rejected any further contact with his wife, and he moved out of town.

Jackson set up a private law business and became district attorney for several counties. In this role, Jackson faced a situation where debtors had banded together to defy the law. Individual defiance of the law was unacceptable to the young lawyer, and group defiance was even worse. He issued over seventy warrants in one month and quickly earned a reputation as a powerhouse of energy and determination. He was named United States Attorney General for the Southwest Territory, an area south of the Ohio River.

As frontiersmen became bolder in claiming land for themselves, Native American tribes hardened their stand against encroachment on their territory, especially the land around the Cumberland River. Members of these tribes carried out raid after raid up and down the river, burning and pillaging. William Blount, governor of the territory south of the Ohio River, gave Jackson orders to enforce a treaty recently signed by the Cherokee leaders. The provisions of the treaty not only limited the Cherokee geographically and politically, it also grossly infringed on their human rights. Jackson led militia teams on expeditions to rout out the tribes. He believed that they needed to be disciplined and punished like children. He spoke against peace talks because, he said, "I fear that their Peace Talks are only Delusions, and in order to put us off our Guard . . . [the entire Indian nation] ought to be Scurged for the infringement of the treaty." Jackson was a strong leader, pushing his troops to ford streams, hack their way through forests, and to attack boldly. More than once, he risked his life to warn other whites of impending attack.

The way that Andrew Jackson and Rachel Donelson Robards were married created a great deal of pain and confusion in their lives. After Lewis Robards deserted Rachel and filed a petition for divorce, she and Jackson were married. Jackson claimed that they thought they were free to marry. But why a trained lawyer would not know the difference between a petition for divorce and the granting of a divorce was never explained. After living two years as husband and wife they learned that the divorce had just been granted. This meant thier earlier marriage was not legal. They quickly remarried, but the damage was done. For the remainder of his life Jackson's enemies spread rumors that were the cause of at least two duels he fought.

In December 1793, Governor Blount led a campaign to have Tennessee admitted to the Union. Jackson became one of five members of a convention committee created to draft a preliminary constitution. His support of a provision giving all free white men the right to vote led to his reputation as a champion of the masses. He supported full government participation in removing Native Americans from any area where whites wanted to live. He called for establishment of a legislature to be known as the General Assembly and a Bill of Rights to insure freedom of speech, press and assembly as well as trial by jury for white males. He became known for opening his remarks on any subject by saying that he had the good of the country at heart.

Maybe the story that Jackson named Tennessee is true. That tale says that Jackson chose the Cherokee word meaning the Great

Governor William Blount led a campaign to make the Tennessee territory a state.

Crooked River because "it has a flavor on the tongue as sweet as hot corn-cakes and honey."

On June 1, 1796, President George Washington signed the bill that made Tennessee the sixteenth state. Twenty-nine-year-old Andrew Jackson was elected as Tennessee's only representative to the House of Representatives. For the swearing-in ceremony in Philadelphia, the frontier militia man exchanged his casual dress for a brand new black cloth coat with a velvet collar and Florentine breeches. He became a member of a legislature that represented the five million inhabitants of the new nation.

Although he was new to Congress, he questioned President George Washington's authority. He declared that the first president had "been Grasping after power, and in many circumstances, Exercised power that he was not Constitutionally invested with." He did back Washington, however, in December 1796 when the president sponsored a bill to pay state militias to continue their battles with Indian tribes. The bill passed with Jackson's help, and the new representative secured a strong position in the hearts of Tennesseans.

Some reports say that during this time Jackson engaged in slave trading, a very lucrative business in Tennessee in the last half of the eighteenth century. Records reveal that Jackson was a shrewd land speculator and took advantage of the buying and selling of hundreds of acres along the frontier. These transactions forced him to be away from home a lot of the time. He assured Rachel in every letter," My heart rests with you ... I mean to retire from the Buss of publick life, and Spend my Time with you alone in Sweet Retirement, which is My only ambition and ultimate wish."

Chapter Two

The Threat of Inaction

Retirement was not in the cards for Representative Andrew Jackson. He was elected to the Senate by the Tennessee legislature. William Cocke, the other senatorial candidate, also won. Jackson believed that Cocke had betrayed him by revealing the contents of a private letter. He challenged Cocke to a duel, citing "the opprobrium that has been attached to my character upon false evidence [and] must be publickly washed away . . ." Just before the duel was scheduled, both men agreed that the whole situation was a mere misunderstanding, saving their honor, and possibly their lives.

Jackson's temper led him into conflict with Vice-President Thomas Jefferson who wrote of him: "His passions are terrible . . . he could never speak on account of the rashness of his feelings." Jackson's career in the Senate was not a happy one. He was bored with long discussions and frustrated by what he considered the inefficiency of the federal government. Besides, he was plagued by debts incurred in land speculation, and Senate attendance kept him from taking care of his business matters. He missed Rachel, and Rachel frequently showed her displeasure at his absence. In April 1798, he resigned his seat, giving no apology or explanation.

Then he asked the legislature to elect him to a seat on the state superior court, a position which paid $600 a year. They did so, and Jackson became the second highest paid official in Tennessee, second only to the governor who made $750. In his new position, he traveled widely throughout the state. He was amazed at the changes that had occurred in the few years since he first came to Tennessee. Many new towns had arisen on the banks of the Mississippi and inland. Log cabins were still popular, but now frame houses dotted the rolling hills, too. An increasing number of shops carried silks and brocades and other elegant merchandise. The area was moving quickly from its frontier beginnings to becoming a settled society. Jackson held the post for six years and earned a favorable reputation for his integrity, his swift and fair decisions, and his strong sense of justice.

Jackson gained more notoriety when Russell Bean was arrested for cutting off the ears of an infant in a drunken stupor. Bean arrived on the court house steps but refused to enter the court. Neither a sheriff nor a posse could force him up the steps. Jackson left the court, approached the defendant with a pistol in each hand, and told him to get inside or be shot. Bean entered the court. When asked later why he had obeyed Jackson when he ignored an entire posse, Bean replied that he could tell after one glance into his eyes that Justice Jackson would shoot him. With his reputation for toughness, it is not surprising that Jackson was elected major general of the Tennessee militia.

Because Rachel's divorce from Lewis Robards and her subsequent marriage to Jackson were never recorded, some who disliked Jackson accused him of having an adulterous affair with Rachel. One of these people was gubernatorial candidate John Sevier. Sevier was angry because Jackson had testified against him

Jackson challenged John Sevier to a duel in 1803.

in a fraud case. In response to Sevier's allegations, Jackson challenged him to a duel: "I shall expect to see you with your friend and no other person. My friend and myself will be armed with pistols . . ." The duel was set for October 12, 1803. With pistol ready, Jackson waited, and waited, and waited. Sevier showed up two days after the agreed-upon date. The two men cursed, threatened each other with guns and a sword, but did not fight a duel.

Jackson formed a partnership with two other men to operate a cotton gin, a distillery, and some stores which sold staples like coffee, blankets, dry goods, and gunpowder. For the most part, customers paid in cotton, tobacco, pork, furs, and other goods rather than in money. While Jackson was busy in the store, Rachel managed the approximately twenty slaves who worked the cotton, corn, and wheat crops on their farm. Jackson ordered that his slaves be treated humanely, but he used whips and chains when he suspected laziness, incompetence, or hostility. He bred horses, cows, and mules and was particularly proud of his champion race horses. He also took his birds to cockfights. He continued to speculate in land despite many problems with deeds and payments.

Land ownership was not just a problem for Jackson; it was also a problem for the federal government as the new country tested its boundaries. Conflict between the Spanish and the French in Louisiana heated up. The French leader Napoleon Bonaparte forced the Spanish to cede disputed territory to France. The United States then bought that land from Napoleon. Jackson believed that his firm hand was needed to guide the citizens away from French and Spanish influence and into the traditions of the new United States. He applied for appointment as governor and set to work to convince the Tennessee Congressional delegation to support him. He was angry when Jefferson chose W. C. C. Claiborne over him.

Jackson became involved in another dispute that led to a another duel challenge. Again, the subject was Rachel and the legitimacy of their marriage. Jackson accused Charles Dickinson, a young lawyer, of making insulting remarks about Rachel. When faced with the facts, Dickinson apologized. But then he put himself in the middle of a conflict between Jackson and a man who owed Jackson money. Dickinson told the man that Jackson was a lying scoundrel and a coward. Jackson sent Dickinson a letter saying, "Your conduct and expressions, relative to me of late have been of such a nature and so insulting, that it requires and shall have my notice."

A duel was set for May 30, 1806. A crowd eagerly awaited the match with most people betting on Dickinson to be the better shot. The attending surgeon handed each man his weapon, a pistol with a nine-inch barrel that shot one ounce balls. The men took their places twenty-four feet apart. Dickinson's first shot hit Jackson in the chest. As he fell, Jackson shot and hit Dickinson in the ribs. Dickinson fell. With both men on the ground, the surgeon announced that the duel was over.

Other men carried Dickinson away. As Jackson got up, his supporters noticed a red stain on his chest, Jackson closed his coat quickly saying that he did not want anyone to know he was hurt. A doctor told Jackson that Dickinson's bullet had shattered two of his ribs and lodged in his chest. Because it was so close to the heart, the bullet could not be removed. Dickinson died a couple of hours later.

In 1804, Jackson bought a 420-acre site near Nashville that he named the Hermitage. He and Rachel moved into the two-story blockhouse on the land. The first story was a single room with a fireplace for cooking and heating. At the Hermitage, which Jackson called a farm, the couple entertained frequently. Jackson was a good conversationalist. He listened well, had an entertaining sense of humor, and gave his opinion freely and politely.

One famous guest was Aaron Burr, former vice-president of the United States, who went into hiding after he was indicted for the murder of Secretary of the Treasury Alexander Hamilton. Now he was back, and Jackson enlisted his help in routing out Spanish forces in parts of Florida, Texas, Mexico, and other land reaching as far west as California. Jackson declared that the Spanish presence was humiliating to the United States.

He helped Burr to acquire some large boats and to supply them with provisions. He wrote to General James Winchester that with "less than two million [dollars] we can conquer not only the florida, but all Spanish North America." He offered another temptation: "Should there be a war, it will be a handsome theatre for our enterprising young men, and a source of acquiring fame."

He heard a rumor that Burr planned to take New Orleans and then Louisiana and then the whole country for himself. The rumor also reported that General James Wilkinson, commanding general of the United States army in the lower Mississippi valley, was scheming to help Burr. Unwilling to tolerate the slightest hint of treason, Jackson dashed off warning letters to political friends. He did not name Burr, but he urged that measures be taken to ward off possible danger. To be fair, he also wrote to Burr and asked him outright for his pledge not to act against the Union. Burr assured him that he had no intention of any such action. Jackson weighed the anti-Burr rumors against the declaration of his friend and fellow soldier. He accepted Burr's declaration of innocence.

Jackson testified against Aaron Burr in 1807.

President Jefferson did not agree. He ordered Jackson to ready his men for attack against Burr. An obedient soldier, Jackson called out the troops, drilled them in public places, and passed on his energy and optimism. The drills created an efficient regiment, and the enthusiasm generated a loyal following among civilians in the area. It also served a third, and more important, purpose. It alerted Burr, who actually had prepared to attack the Union. Burr disappeared, deserting his men and boats.

Burr was captured by U. S. forces and put on trial for treason in the spring of 1807. Jackson took the stand as a witness to Burr's treachery. Despite Jackson's testimony, the jury found Burr not guilty. The exonerated man fled to Europe.

The news was full of stories about Jackson's rages against Burr. Reporters eagerly added other incidents, or fabricated incidents, illustrating Jackson's temper tantrums and bouts of anger. Historians are divided in their opinions. Some think that Jackson was simply an extremely hot-tempered person. Others think that he was always totally in control and that he exploited his reputation for anger to make a point dramatically and to intimidate his opposition.

Back at the Hermitage, Jackson spent several years tending crops, buying and selling slaves and land, and keeping up his stable of racing horses. He became a well-to-do farmer with many friends and acquaintances. He boasted about his military past: "My pride is that my soldiers have complete confidence in me, and on the event of a war I will lead them on to victory and conquest." His entertaining kept him in touch with important politicians and strengthened his political standing in western Tennessee. Despite all this activity, Jackson lived with continual health problems. He suffered periodically from fevers, a result of the smallpox he contracted when he was a child. Chronic dysentery, a painful diarrhea, also plagued him. The wound he received from Dickinson brought recurring discomfort and congestion.

A devoted wife, Rachel helped him as much as she could. She was a lively and vivacious hostess, and she impressed friends and visitors with her intelligence. Her openness earned her the nickname of Aunt Rachel. As time went on, she became immersed in her religion. Because of several miscarriages and infant deaths, the couple had no children. But they both became very close to the children of their relatives and their friends. In 1809, they adopted one of a set of twins born to Rachel's sister-in-law, a boy whom they named Andrew Jackson, Jr. The couple also took in John, Daniel, and Andrew Donelson (more of Rachel's nephews) whose father had died; William Smith, the son of neighbors who could not care for him; and various nieces and nephews as they saw a need.

Despite his success with the Hermitage, Jackson was dissatisfied with his life. He saw serious potential problems in the country. Conflict with the British was heating up again. The Native American situation remained an undeclared war. Spanish-American hostility increased. Jackson considered himself to be a soldier without a war, and he declared that "As a military man...indolence and inaction would shortly destroy me."

Although the United States was a new country, the government wanted to show the world that it was already a strong nation. Also, United States leaders wanted possession of Canadian land to expand economic opportunity and to remove forever any chance of British attack on the northern border. The British navy had been seizing American ships, and British agents encouraged Indian raids along the borders. A group of congressman called the War Hawks, led by two young representatives named Henry Clay of Kentucky and John Calhoun of South Carolina, demanded that Great Britian be made to show respect for the new nation.

When, in June 1812, President Madison asked Congress for a declaration of war against Great Britain, forty-five-year-old Jackson put out his own call for troops in a proclamation and posters: "VOLUNTEERS TO ARMS! . . . We are going to fight for the reestablishment of our national character." He immediately offered the president 2500 volunteers ready to fight and die for the cause. While he waited for the president's answer, Jackson organized and drilled the troops. He also outfitted them, using his own money when necessary. For months, happy to be doing what he loved best, Jackson and his soldiers drilled.

Chapter Three

Compelled from Duty

The orders that finally came from President Madison were both good news and bad news for Jackson. The good news was that his troops would, at last, be able to fight for their country against the British. The bad news was that his regiments would be under the command of Brigadier General Wilkinson, the leader who had schemed with Burr and had only narrowly escaped the condemnation that Burr had faced. Jackson agreed to serve under Wilkinson on one condition: That they would both bring along their dueling pistols, just in case trouble arose between them.

When Governor Blount was authorized to supply volunteers for an expedition to New Orleans, he named Jackson a major general of those volunteers. Major General Jackson eagerly answered the call of his country: "At a period like the present, it is the duty of every citizen to do something for his country . . . I will sacrifice my own feelings . . ." His wife, Rachel, warned him: "Do not, my beloved husband let the love of country, fame and honor, make you forget you have [a wife]."

In December 1812, Jackson advised his troops to prepare for a five-or six-month expedition. He told them to bring their own rifles. They set off in foot-deep snow, Jackson encouraging the men every step of the way. When praised for his fine troops, Jackson answered that he felt fortunate to live in a republic and that fighting for this government was a duty he owed to his country and to future generations of Americans. Any sacrifice was merely a reflection of his responsibility to duty.

They spent thirty-nine days traveling down the ice-clogged Ohio River, losing three men and one boat before they landed in Natchez, a thousand miles from Nashville. There Jackson received several notes from Wilkinson, advising him to stay in Natchez. He also received a letter from Rachel which said, in part: "my blessed Redeemer is making intercession with the Father for us to meet again..."

For weeks as Jackson waited for word to move, both he and his troops became more and more restless. In March he received a letter from Secretary of War John Armstrong ordering him to disband his regiment since they were no longer needed. Jackson exploded in rage. He was in wilderness Indian country, 500 miles from home, without transport or medicine. How could he disband 2000 men under these circumstances? He suspected that General Wilkinson had a part in this order. He also suspected that a cowardly Congress feared the Spanish and did not dare continue with the scheduled attacks.

Jackson refused to obey the order to disband. He said he would lead his soldiers back home to Tennessee. If necessary, he would pay the soldiers himself since they had followed him loyally, and he would see that they arrived home safely. He wrote letters to political and military officials, cursing both President Madison and General Wilkinson who, he said, were "...hypocritical Political Villains, who would sacrifice the best blood of our Country."

The trip from Natchez to Nashville strengthened the already

Brigadier General James Wilkinson was supposed to have command over Jackson and his regiment during their march to New Orleans.

strong bond between Jackson and his troops, and it demonstrated his willpower. The men were tired and hungry, their march was long, and their spirits were failing. With 156 soldiers on the sick-list, only eleven wagons and severely rationed food, Jackson gently prodded his men to persevere. They described him as tough, tough as hickory. Some began to call him Hickory. Thus, Major General Andrew Jackson became beloved "Old Hickory."

Within a month, Jackson had his troops back in Tennessee. The *Nashville Whig* headlined "Long will their General live in the memory of his volunteers of West Tennessee, for his benevolence, humane, and fatherly treatment to his soldiers . . ."

After he had returned home with his men, Thomas Hart Benton, a well-known lawyer, accused Jackson of allowing a duel to take place among his troops. His brother Jesse Benton had been one of the duelists. The lawyer said that his brother had been seriously wounded and that the duel had been savage, unfair, and cruel. Jackson denied the allegations, and he threatened to horsewhip Thomas Benton if he saw him. Benton went to Nashville with his brother Jesse to hunt Jackson down.

The three men met on a public sidewalk. Brandishing a whip, Old Hickory backed the Benton brothers into a hotel. Jesse ducked into a hotel hallway. From this hiding place, he fired at Jackson, hitting him in the arm and shoulder. Jackson fell, firing at Thomas as he went down. He missed. Thomas fired twice more at Jackson who was still on the floor. Onlookers finally stopped the fighting.

Jackson, half conscious, was taken to the Nashville Inn where his blood soaked through two mattresses. In a daze, Jackson heard the doctors talk about amputating his arm. "I'll keep my arm," he ordered from the bed just before he slipped out of consciousness.

The doctors obeyed. They dressed his wounds with poultices of elm and other healing plants. Below them in the streets, crowds shouted at Thomas Benton. Thomas responded that he wanted to have another chance at Jackson. He fled, and their shouts followed him.

Before Jackson completely recovered from his wounds, he entered into the increasing conflicts between white men and Native Americans. The Creek Indians, so nicknamed because they tended to live and hunt on creeks and rivers, massacred white settlers after those settlers had taken some of their land. They attacked other natives in Florida with arms the Spanish had outfitted them with. The British also offered to help the Creeks. So did members of the Shawnee tribe under their chief Tecumseh who insisted that "The Great Spirit gave this land to his red children." Tecumseh had no patience with the situation: "Let the white race perish! They seize your land; they corrupt your women; they trample on the bones of your dead!" First some of the Creeks and then members of other tribes began to fear that Tecumseh's desire for retaliation might do more harm than good. Soon the Native Americans were in a kind of civil war between the tribes.

In August 1813, a thousand Creeks rushed into a white settlement near Mobile under Chief Red Eagle. They slaughtered 250 white settlers. Chickasaw leaders, fearing retribution by the whites, demanded that the Creeks punish those who had taken part in the massacre. The Creeks did so, but the punishment served to widen the civil war among Native American tribes.

Tennesseans called on Old Hickory to rush to Alabama and destroy the Creeks. Jackson was more than ready. He was unwilling to wait for official orders from Blount. From his sickbed, he sent orders to his militia to report to Fayetteville for immediate duty. "We must not await the slow and tardy orders of the General Government . . . The health of your general is restored, he will command in person."

Jackson planned that he and his men would drive through the Creek nation, building a road through the wilderness as they went. Then he would invade Florida and capture Pensacola from the Spanish. Thus, he would accomplish three goals: Eliminate the Spanish from the southern frontier, eliminate the Native Americans from Florida, and construct a road for westward expansion.

His arm still in a sling, Jackson led his troops at a speedy pace of thirty-six miles a day to the southern tip of the Tennessee River. He estimated that his troops could easily consume ten wagon loads of food a day, a thousand barrels of grain a week, and tons of meat. He built a supply station he named Fort Deposit, hoping to receive the supplies he had ordered, but he was too impatient to wait for them. Old Hickory ordered his troops to march ahead, foraging in villages when possible, existing on acorns and other forest food when they needed to.

A few days later, Jackson led his men in an attack on a Creek village. They killed 186 braves and captured eighty-four women and children. When the captured Creeks refused to take care of an infant named Lyncoya who was orphaned by the raid, he cared for the boy himself. As soon as he could, he sent Lyncoya to the Hermitage with instructions that he be treated like Jackson's own son.

In a battle at Talledega, Jackson's troops killed 300 Creeks. His losses were fifteen dead and eighty-five wounded. There was no doubt that Major General Jackson's troops, supplies, and military expertise were far superior to the Creeks.

Despite the victories, Old Hickory's soldiers rebelled against

Shawnee Chief Tecumseh demanded revenge against the American government.

the lack of food and medicine. They presented him with a petition in which they demanded to go home. He rejected the petition, reminding his soldiers that they were expected to be loyal. The complaints grew. Soldiers wrote home saying that more troops were deserting every day. Finally Jackson gave an ultimatum. He promised that the soldiers could go back home if supplies did not arrive in two days. The two days passed with no supplies.

Jackson said he would release the men, but he himself would not leave. He asked for two men to volunteer to stay with him. One hundred nine soldiers volunteered. The rest left, promising to return with supplies if they found any. They found their supply train not twelve miles from Fort Deposit. They returned to Jackson with 150 cows for slaughter and nine wagons of flour. They had not been back long before some soldiers again threatened to leave.

Jackson faced the would-be deserters, holding his musket ready. He said the first man to leave for Tennessee would get a bullet in his brain. For minutes, no one moved. Then, slowly but surely the men returned to camp. More supplies arrived, and Jackson breathed a sigh of relief. But on December 10, 1813, the one-year anniversary of their enlistment, volunteers declared that they were free to go. Old Hickory countered that they had spent some of that year just waiting to be called up and besides, he could win the war in a few weeks if they would only hold on. He praised his soldiers for their past service, spoke about the disgrace that fell on deserters, and warned them they would leave only over his dead body.

There was no sound from the troops. He ordered his loyal gunners to light their matches in preparation for shooting. Then a few officers stepped forward to pledge that they would stay until reinforcements arrived. Convinced that the rest would follow their lead, Old Hickory left the scene. He wrote to his wife: "I felt the pangs of an effecitonate parent, compelled from duty to chastise his child—to prevent him from destruction & disgrace."

Jackson was not the only American officer to have such problems with the troops, but he was more successful than many at keeping his force together. American soldiers were faring badly throughout the states and territories. In army camp after army camp, they were attacked by Native American tribes who sought retaliation. Mass desertions of American troops followed massacres by native tribes. A few white citizens objected to the treatment of Native Americans, but they were scarcely heard.

Finally, Jackson's reinforcements arrived, and the First Brigade left for home. Old Hickory discovered that the newly arrived replacements would complete their terms of service to the military within a few days. These men had enlisted for just three months under the regulations of the Tennessee legislature. Jackson objected. He said that federal regulations did not accept enlistments of less than six months, and therefore, they were still on duty. Blount and Secretary of War Armstrong said that states' rights superceded federal rights. Blount ordered Old Hickory to retreat to the Tennessee frontier and free the troops.

Jackson refused. He told him that the Choctaws could be beaten: "You have only to act with a little energy for which you will be applauded by your Government. Give me a force for 6 months . . . and all may be safe. Withhold it, and all is lost . . ." He told his troops what he had written to Blount, and he gave them the choice of staying or leaving. Most of them chose to leave. For weeks he sat in his fort with just 100 men, waiting for replacements.

In January 1814, 800 recruits marched into that fort. Old Hickory was so delighted that he kept them marching straight into

Creek country. There was heavy fighting with many casualties. Jackson's troops succeeded in driving off the enemy. After the smoke died down, Old Hickory proudly complimented his volunteers for their bravery and skill. "The gratitude of a country of freemen is yours; yours the applause of an admiring world!"

He insisted that his troops be on duty by 3:00 each morning in order to prevent surprise attacks. This was harsh discipline for new recruits who were hungry, far from home, and afraid. But Old Hickory feared that he would face organized opposition if he wavered in his demands. When an eighteen-year-old soldier was arrested for failing to obey orders, most of the troops believed the young soldier's story that he had been given contradictory orders. Jackson ordered the young man shot by firing squad. This act intensified the spirit of mutiny that bubbled just below the surface in most recruits. On the other hand, it drove this spirit underground for fear of punishment.

In March 1814, his spies told General Jackson that the Creeks were gathering at an area called Horseshoe Bend, a peninsula in the Tallapoosa River. The Creeks, sometimes called Red Sticks because they painted their war clubs red, met to protect the land which they believed to be sacred. Jackson marched 2500 men to the Horseshoe Bend and set up guns aimed at the camp. For two hours, the artillery fired into the camp every time a Creek poked out his head. Then some of Jackson's troops set fire to huts grouped around the edge of the camp. The fires distracted the Creeks long enough to allow Jackson's men to charge into the compound.

Old Hickory sent an interpreter to ask them to lay down their arms. They refused. The killing continued until the soldiers could no longer see their targets in the waning daylight. The next morning,

Creek Chief Red Eagle surrendered to Jackson at Horseshoe Bend.

Jackson ordered his men to take count of the Native American dead by cutting off the tips of their noses. They counted 560 dead Creeks on the ground and about 300 bodies in the river. They took 300 captives. Creek Chief Red Eagle surrendered to Old Hickory without a fight. He came to Jackson saying, "I am in your power....I can now do no more than weep over the misfortunes of my nation."

On April 18, Jackson reported to Blount that the Creek War was over. Everywhere he went, Jackson was praised for his determination and courage. And everywhere he went, Jackson praised his men for the same qualities. "The bravery you have displayed in the field of battle, and the uniform good conduct . . . will long be cherished in the memory of your general, and will not be forgotten by the country you have so materially benefitted."

Just eight months after he had left his sickbed to take up leadership of his troops, he was greeted as a hero. He accepted promotion to general. That was the good news. The bad news was that the Old Hickory suffered from diarrhea and dysentery, a shattered bone from the remains of the bullet in his arm, and general weakness due to the strain of eight month's battle with insufficient food, clothing, and shelter. Physically he was weak; emotionally he was stronger than he had ever been.

He was ordered to conclude a peace treaty with the Creeks. He demanded that all Creek leaders surrender to him on August 1, 1814.

The chiefs appeared and were told to stand at one side of a large canopy. Jackson and his men stood at the other. Jackson opened the meeting with a little praise for friendly Creeks and a scolding for militant Red Sticks. He told them they owed the United States reparations for war damages. The "bill" was about half of their territory: 23 million acres of land in Alabama and Georgia. Three more demands included: Stop all communication with the

British and the Spanish, acknowledge the right of United States citizens to travel freely through Native American territory, force their chiefs to surrender to Jackson. After the Creek interpreters translated Jackson's speech, the chiefs retired to a private council.

A few days later, the chiefs accepted the terms. To make sure the Creeks did not try to find refuge in Florida, Jackson sent a message to the Spanish governor of Pensacola, warning him not to help the Creeks. He said that the United States would retaliate against Spain if necessary: "An Eye for an Eye Toothe for Toothe and Scalp for Scalp." Within a generation, Creeks, Cherokees, Chickasaws, Choctaws, and Seminoles were virtually banished from the South. General Jackson was enormously proud of himself. He believed that the treaty was fair to both red men and white men. He had proven that Native Americans could be dealt with by regulation and punishment. He also believed that he had squelched any possible cooperation between Native Americans and the Spanish.

Chapter Four

The Battle of New Orleans

Despite Jackson's assurance that the new American government could dominate its enemies, the United States still faced many problems. To begin with, some white citizens were aghast at Jackson's treatment of Native Americans. And to make matters worse, the British were on a rampage. They burned the president's mansion and the capitol in Washington City, shelled Baltimore, and marched into New York. Through his spies, General Jackson learned of their plans to capture Mobile, Alabama, and then to move on to surrounding areas. He rushed his troops to Mobile, declaring that he wanted revenge against the British.

His spies did not pick up the information that the British had changed their plans. Jackson waited, sure the attack would come. Soon he became restless and decided to invade Florida to restrict Spanish power there. Secretary of War James Monroe, who was also Secretary of State, sent Jackson word that the British planned to take New Orleans. He ordered him to prepare for this attack. But even as Monroe was writing that letter, Jackson was planning to invade Florida whether he received specific orders to do so or not.

On October 25, Jackson wrote to Monroe that he was acting

without presidential orders, and therefore, he wanted to explain his reasons for the action. He said that his move to Florida was necessary to stop the Spanish governor of Pensacola from persuading Native Americans and the British to help him fight against the United States. Monroe did not respond.

A little more than two weeks later, Jackson arrived in Pensacola, a town that consisted mostly of two small forts. He sent a note to Governor Gonzalez Manrique, telling him that he wanted immediate possession of Fort Barrancas, the fort that guarded the bay. He would keep control until the Spanish proved that they would be neutral in the conflict between the United States and Britain. "If my demands are rejected," he wrote, "I will not hold myself responsible for the conduct of my enraged soldiers."

For some unknown reason, Governor Manrique did not receive the letter. Someone (historians suspect the British) fired on the truce flag that Jackson flew. At the first shot, Old Hickory ordered his troops to attack, and American soldiers poured into Pensacola. Within a few minutes, Governor Manrique appeared with a white flag. The British hastily retreated. Content that the British would not return and that the Spanish would no longer violate their neutrality, Jackson turned Pensacola back over to Governor Manrique. Jackson's status as a military hero grew and so did the loyalty of the men who fought under him

General Jackson planned to meet the next British assault at New Orleans. He wrote to Rachel, begging her to come and bring Andrew, Jr. He told her he had found a beautiful Spanish-style house on the gulf with a garden of hyacinths and mimosa trees. He needed her, he said, and was on the verge of collapse. According to two of his colleagues, General Jackson's "complexion was sallow and unhealthy . . . his body thin and emaciated."

On November 27, an armada of sixty British ships carrying 14,000 British troops headed for New Orleans. Jackson spoke to the citizens of that city using a French interpreter. He urged them to unite against the British, and he immediately began preparations for their defense. He needed to cut down trees to block the many bayous that could serve as highways. He had to strengthen the forts along the river. He also made a deal with pirate Jean Laffite who had a thousand men, heavy guns, powder, shot, and a reputation for excellent marksmanship. Laffite offered Jackson the support of his troops in return for an amnesty for their acts of piracy. The deal was made. A group of free blacks also offered their help, and Jackson accepted. This deal stirred distrust among many Louisiana whites who feared trouble if blacks were given arms. General Jackson responded: "Be pleased to keep to yourself your opinions upon the policy . . . [of filling] the necessary muster roles without inquiring whether the troops are white, black or tea."

The British were sighted just off New Orleans on December 13, 1814. They attacked and defeated the American naval force that tried to prevent them from entering the bay south of the city. Jackson ordered all troops possible to come to New Orleans to assist him. He sent the message that they were not to rest until they were within striking distance. He told Governor Claiborne that he needed to impose martial law on the city, giving himself the rights to draft men into his army and to question and detain any suspected spies. Governor Claiborne agreed, but the legislature rejected the idea.

Nevertheless, on December 16, Jackson declared martial law in the city. On December 18, he spoke both to his soldiers and to the assembled crowd. He told them that the enemy was very near, but that he knew the brave soldiers and citizens were united.

Pirate Jean Laffite aided Jackson in the Battle of New Orleans.

On December 22, a well-equipped British flotilla moved toward the bayous that surrounded New Orleans. Only one bayou was not adequately protected by Americans, and the British found it. When Jackson learned that the flotilla was about nine miles from the city and moving forward, he shouted, "By the Eternal, they shall not sleep on our soil! . . . I will smash them, so help me God!" He did not smash them, but he brought them to a standstill.

On December 25, the fighting in New Orleans accelerated. Jackson received word that the Louisiana legislature was ready to surrender. Old Hickory told Governor Claiborne that any legislator who showed the least inclination toward surrender would be arrested and jailed. He said that if retreat should become necessary he would destroy the city to keep it out of British hands. For several days, Americans and British traded shots from boats, banks, swamps, and fields. Jackson ordered his men to build the highest rampart they could, a wall of mud and dirt high enough to shield soldiers from the shots of the 24-pounders and 12-pounders that the British were pouring onto the city. He told citizens to gather every available sword, pistol, and musket, and to be ready for hand-to-hand combat.

On New Year's Day, Jackson put on another public military review. His troops were a ragtag bunch of regular militia, pirates, and free blacks, united by Jackson's charisma. Bands played, officers rode through ranks of soldiers, and flags waved. Suddenly the British fired. Rockets burst into the scene. Jackson rushed his men to the ramparts, coaxing "Don't mind these rockets, they are mere toys to amuse children." In just a few minutes, Jackson had his troops at the ramparts, ready to meet the British charge.

More days of fighting took place. Jackson wrote to President Madison, begging for more arms and supplies. He complained about Madison's failure to support the troops: "This supineness, this negligence, this *criminality*, let me call it, of which we witness so many instances in the agents of Government, must finally lead, if not corrected, to the defeat of our armies." Finally some replacement troops did arrive, but most of these men had no arms. Day after day Jackson's troops waited and listened to sounds from the British camp. They heard the steady beat of marching soldiers, the drone of bagpipes, and the clunk and thump of axes cutting down cypress trees to make barricades.

In the early morning of January 8, 1815, only a thick mist separated the two armies. As the haze lifted, rockets shot across the fields from both sides, some exploding in the air and raining shrapnel, some exploding on the ground a few seconds after landing. Jackson darted through the smoke and haze, a tall figure in a long blue cloak, encouraging his troops. The firing increased, and Jackson posed on a hill in view of as many men as possible, sitting proudly and confidently on his horse. Finally the British beat a retreat, leaving a battle field crowded with body upon body. Someone said that a person could walk on corpses for half a mile and never touch the ground.

The east bank of the Mississippi was safe under American command. Jackson reviewed the cheering troops as the band played "Hail Columbia." He accepted the applause of his soldiers with the modest disclaimer that it was divine providence that had shielded his men from the bombs and rockets and that had guided the shots of the American soldiers directly into the enemy camp.

Battle records show about 50 Americans dead or wounded, and about 2000 British dead or wounded. At first, Jackson could not believe these figures. But re-counting made little difference in the statistics. Old Hickory declared that the counting was correct, and that the American soldiers had won decisively. Jackson's massive fire power at the precise time and place was responsible for the one-sided victory.

On the west bank of the Mississippi, the scene was entirely different. When British officers attacked, the Americans retreated en masse, unable or unwilling to listen to the pleas of their officers to return and fight. Jackson faced those who had run from battle. He blamed them for their defeat: "How then Could brave men abandon the post committed to their care. The want of Discipline, the want of Order, a total disregard to Obedience, and a Spirit of insubordination . . . this appears to be the cause which led to the disaster."

Then he returned to the troops he had led in the victory on the east bank. On January 23, he made a triumphal entrance into the center of the city square. He grandly marched under a temporary arch built just for the celebration. People cheered wildly as the Hero of the Battle of New Orleans strode through the arch with his staff. On his way to a church, a group of young girls recited: "Hail to the chief! who hied at war's alarm/ to save our threaten'd land from hostile arms . . ." Jackson answered that he could seek no higher blessing from heaven than to have helped free his country from the enemy.

Citizens of New Orleans demonstrated wildly for Jackson— until he re-imposed martial law, explaining that it was necessary to retain military preparedness as long as the British fleet was in the gulf. Once again, citizens were subject to the draft, to arrest on charges of spying, and to curfew. They put down their flags and banners and demonstrated against Jackson. Overnight, Andrew Jackson the Hero of New Orleans became Andrew Jackson the tyrant.

On February 4, news of the victory at New Orleans reached Washington. Headlines shouted the news, singling out Jackson as their hero. Rachel and little Andrew left the Hermitage to join him. Just nine days later, news came across the Atlantic that American and British foreign ministers had signed a peace treaty in Ghent, Belgium.

When news of the treaty of Ghent reached New Orleans, citizens there demanded an end to martial law. Jackson refused. He would not change a single regulation until he received official confirmation of the treaty from the government, not from a newspaper. Instead of being more lenient, he tightened his policies. When Louis Louailler, a journalist and member of the Louisiana legislature, publicly demanded an end to martial law, Jackson had him arrested. Federal Judge Dominick Hall defended Louailler. Jackson had the judge arrested for treason. At a trial, the journalist was acquitted. Jackson was not satisfied. He sent Louailler back to jail.

On March 13, 1815, official verification of the peace treaty arrived in New Orleans. Immediately, Jackson revoked martial law, pardoned all who were accused of military offenses, and dismissed the militia and volunteers. For the second time that year, New Orleans celebrated its freedom—this time from General Andrew Jackson.

At last Rachel, Andrew, and little Andrew were free to go back to the Hermitage. Forty-seven-year-old Rachel and the forty-eight-year-old general made quite a picture. He was tall, lanky, and sophisticated. She was plump, socially awkward, and plain in dress. Five-year-old Little Andrew was a joy to both parents. Old Hickory showered his adopted son with attention and gifts.

Jackson's name was not easily forgiven in New Orleans. Judge

Hall demanded that the Hero of New Orleans be brought to trial for his imposition of martial law. The accusation read in part: "We are compelled, therefore, to attribute the arbitrary proceedings of the defendant, not to his conviction of their necessity, but to the indulged infirmity of an obstinate and morbidly irascible temperament, and to the unyielding pride of a man naturally impatient of the least show of opposition to his will."

The case of *United States v. Major General Andrew Jackson* began on March 24, 1815. Dominick Hall was the presiding judge. In an opening statement, Jackson insisted that the judge should excuse himself because of his prior involvement in the case. Even as he insisted, Jackson admitted defeat, declaring that he knew that the judge would not listen to either reason or argument. At the beginning of the trial, Judge Hall asked Jackson nineteen questions about his reasons for imposing martial law and his actions in connection with that law. Jackson refused to answer any of them, saying that the trial was totally unfair: "Under these circumstances I appear before your Honor to receive the sentence of the court, and with nothing further to add." Judge Hall declared Jackson guilty and said he would waive a prison term in view of the general's service to the country. He imposed a fine of $1000. Jackson paid it. His quiet acceptance of the judge's decision won him friends.

Chapter Five

Brothers, Listen

In May as the small Jackson family made their way back to the Hermitage from New Orleans, they were honored in many cities where citizens competed to pay Andrew Jackson respect. Everywhere he went, the soldiers were among the loudest in their praise for their general. The hero accepted the praise with a modesty that people appreciated, just as they had appreciated his acceptance of the judge's decision.

For a few months, Jackson enjoyed the life of a country gentleman at his plantation. Rachel had done an excellent job of taking care of business matters. The profit from the farm plus his military pay and allowances left him very well off. He spent time with young Andrew and with Lyncoya, the Creek child whom he had rescued. He kept track of the progress of the removal of Native Americans, and he was disturbed by news that some Creeks in Florida were still resisting. He sent them a stern warning: "Brothers, Listen, My men are ready to crush all the enemies of the U. States . . ."

He found strong support for his views in James Monroe, the Democrat who seemed most likely to be the next president. On a tour of the south, Jackson tried again to threaten the Native

Americans into giving up their land. He was enraged when the new Secretary of War, William Crawford, agreed to return four million acres of land to the Cherokees and to compensate them over $25,000 for damages to crops and livestock during the war. General Jackson fired off a letter to Washington threatening to disobey any order that compelled him to help effect this new policy.

Crawford accepted defeat. He appointed a board of three commissioners, including Jackson, to conclude treaties with the Cherokees, Choctaws, and Chickasaws. The general dominated the commission. He said that the Native Americans had no rights except those granted them by Congress. "I conclude that Congress has full power, by law, to regulate all the concerns of the Indians." He also told the commissioners that Indians were never to be trusted.

In September 1816, Cherokee and Chickasaw leaders met with Jackson. Old Hickory's opening speech was warm: "Friends & Brethren ... [I am here] to shake you by the hand, brighten the chain of Friendship & greet you with pleasing tidings that Peace & Friendship exists between the People of the U States & all their red Brethren ..." Then he asked the leaders to present their positions.

The Cherokees spoke first, insisting that they would yield no land. Jackson countered that they had to yield 2 million acres, and that he had prepared a map to define this territory. In return, the Cherokees would receive $6000 a year for ten years plus a bonus of $5000 as soon as they ratified the treaty. On September 14, the Cherokee leaders signed the treaty. Next, Jackson spoke to the leaders of the Chickasaws. He told them they had to yield an area of land which would allow the whites to connect their Tennessee settlements with the Gulf of Mexico. Like the Cherokees, the Chickasaws protested. Also like the Cherokee leaders, the Chickasaw leaders finally signed the treaty which granted them $1200 a year for ten years plus a bonus of $4500 at the time of signing. Negotiations with the Choctaws proceeded along somewhat the same lines.

Thousands of speculators, farmers, adventurers, and squatters rushed into these territories to assert their rights. All of these people felt indebted to Andrew Jackson. But Jackson had not completed his self-assigned mission. He would not rest until the Native Americans kept their promises to move out of all territory east of the Mississippi. It seemed that he could not hear the protests of some citizens against the inhumane treatment of Native Americans. After signing the treaties, sixty-seven Indian chiefs sent a petition to the president protesting the agreements. Jackson went to these leaders and asked them individually if each had signed a treaty. They agreed that they had, but they insisted that they did not understand what the treaties meant. Jackson warned them that they should remember the fate of the Creeks who disobeyed their Father. The chiefs returned to their tribes in despair.

Jackson believed he knew what was best for Indians, and he would see that they received it, even if they had to be punished to accept it. This was the same attitude he had toward his soldiers, and it was a common attitude of whites in the United States against both blacks and Native Americans.

Jackson believed that African Americans, Seminole Indians, and the Spanish in Florida posed threats to American sovereignty. African Americans were a threat because they might retaliate against whites at any time. The Seminoles were a threat because they were helping runaway slaves. The Spanish were a threat because they believed that the Florida territory belonged to them.

Jackson asked President Monroe for permission to attack both the Spanish and the Seminoles.

In early 1818, Jackson authorized his officers to recruit troops from Tennessee. He advanced $4000 of his own money to pay for supplies and equipment. He supplied a quart of corn and three rations of meat for each of his 5000 soldiers, and they set off for a five-day trek over the flooded countryside of Georgia. The troops moved east, destroying tribal villages where they encountered any hint of resistance, seizing cattle and food supplies, and sending hundreds of Native Americans fleeing.

In Florida, he sent a message to a Spanish commander saying that he would take over the fort at St. Marks to use as a base for his troops. The commanding officer, who did not have enough troops to fight back, yielded to Jackson's demands. Then Jackson headed east to the Suwannee River, a hundred miles away. There he hoped to capture the Seminole tribe led by Chief Billy Bowlegs. Jackson was stunned to find the town nearly empty. Then he discovered that British Officers Alexander Arbuthnot and Robert Armbrister had carried advance warning to the Seminoles. He had both men tried in military court for aiding the enemy. When the men were found guilty, Jackson ordered their executions.

Jackson and his troops burned 300 houses and then continued their drive east. They met no resistance. The First Seminole War seemed to have taught the Indians that they could not win against the well-equipped and well-manned troops of the United States. But Jackson took nothing for granted. He guessed that the Seminoles would gather men and supplies in Pensacola. Old Hickory decided to occupy that city to prevent Native Americans from building up an army. He arrived in Pensacola on May 14, 1818, and immediately demanded that Spanish governor José

Seminole Chief Billy Bowlegs evaded Jackson with the aid of two British officers in Florida. Jackson later had the British officers executed for aiding the enemy.

Masot surrender the fort. Masot refused. Jackson ordered his troops to aim their guns at the fort.

After only slight resistance, the Spanish raised a white flag. Jackson occupied the town, stating that in doing so, he had saved helpless women and babies who otherwise would have been butchered by Native Americans. He established martial law in Pensacola. On June 2, he wrote to President Monroe telling him that the American Indian War was over. Then he left for Tennessee, advising the president: "I am at present worn down with fatigue and by a bad cough in my left side which produced a spitting of blood . . . I must have rest." Jackson had gained huge public support for his work both at New Orleans and in Florida, but the price was high. His damaged left arm ached all the time. He coughed often, losing blood when he did. The two bullets still in his body caused recurring problems. He wondered if he could ever regain his health.

Back in Washington City, President Monroe faced international problems, partly because of Jackson's actions in Florida. Under Old Hickory, the United States had seized Spanish property and ousted the Spanish government. Further under Jackson's leadership, two British officers had been executed without an opportunity to get help from their country.

More than six months after Jackson seized control of Pensacola, the president wrote to him telling him that he understood why Jackson had invaded Florida. But, he said, he was worried about the international repercussions. Monroe suggested that Jackson re-write some of the recent Florida history in order to remove any suspicion that Old Hickory had acted beyond the scope of his responsibility. He said that he and his secretary would edit the papers carefully to maintain Jackson's fine reputation. Jackson denied that he had acted without proper authority. He went on to say that he was not afraid of taking responsibility and that he never would be. No! His reports were not to be changed in any way.

The situation did not end there. The Spanish minister to the United States demanded that both Pensacola and St. Marks be restored to Spanish control. He also demanded that Jackson be punished. Secretary of State John Quincy Adams replied that Jackson's actions had been taken against the Seminoles, not against the Spanish.

Once again, conflict swirled around Old Hickory, and once again, Americans took sides for and against him. Politics played an ever increasing role in this conflict as political leaders wondered if Jackson might be a potential candidate for the presidency. Jackson was a center of controversy in Congress too, where representatives debated whether or not he should be tried for disobedience or treason.

In January 1819, the House Committee on Military Affairs investigated the execution of the two British officers near Pensacola and Jackson's seizure of Pensacola and St. Marks. The debates lasted over a month, and the legislature was frequently filled with overflowing crowds eager to hear the arguments.

On February 8, the House voted on three measures: Condemnation of Jackson for the executions of the British officers, declaration of the seizure of Florida as unconstitutional, and censure of Jackson for his imposition of martial law. The House voted "No" on all three measures. Old Hickory gleefully celebrated with his supporters. Everywhere he went he was mobbed by congratulations, cheers, and praise as groups of militia and politicians escorted him through crowds. Bands played "See the Conquering Hero Comes."

His glee was short-lived. In Baltimore, he received bad news about a Senate report. Senators had investigated the Seminole War, just as Representatives had. But where the Representatives had voted to praise, Senate committees heaped criticism and dishonor onto the general. Fortunately for Old Hickory, the Senate adjourned before a vote was taken on the matter. Jackson left Washington City planning revenge against senators whom he believed were responsible for inciting opposition against him.

Jackson's revenge would have to wait. He was exhausted from the political maneuvering and from the emotional swings between adoring fans and revengeful opponents. Besides the emotional strain, he suffered physically. He had never recovered from the dysentery he contracted in the battlefield. His heart sometimes pounded frightfully. He coughed up blood at times. His battle wounds returned in aches and pains, and he frequently needed to use a cane for support. His appetite suffered, and he became emaciated. These problems led to a major collapse when he returned from Washington City in 1819. Many thought he would not live much longer.

For a few months, Andrew rested and recuperated, helped greatly by devoted Rachel. Slowly he regained some of his vitality, and he enjoyed life at the Hermitage. Rachel and Andrew now lived in a large two-story brick house with a sweeping staircase and double porches. Another brick building on the property was a Presbyterian church that Andrew had built for Rachel when she became a member of the congregation. Four hundred acres had been cleared and a formal garden of hedges and flower beds planted. The house was always full of guests—the politicians and soldiers invited by Andrew and the clergymen invited by Rachel.

Jackson did not give in completely to the peaceful life at the Hermitage. He was watching closely when Spain ceded to the United States almost all of their territories east of the Mississippi River in return for a payment of $5 million. He was not pleased that they kept control of Texas. However, he feared that Spain might renegotiate on their promise to leave Florida if they were not allowed this concession in Texas. Both sides expressed satisfaction with the deal.

With Florida now firmly in American control, President Monroe asked Jackson if he would consider accepting the post of governor of that territory, an area of 50,000 square miles. Jackson was not enthusiastic. He reminded Monroe that he was looking forward to retirement, not to another challenge, but he did not completely reject the idea either.

Chapter Six

Not Fit to Be President

Andrew Jackson did not immediatley reject President Monroe's offer to become governor of Florida because of his love for a challenge. Eventually, he had to resign himself to his exhaustion and admit that he could not take the position. He was fatigued; aches and pains plagued him day and night. He had to look to his wife and children, too. He wanted to build a new house for Rachel. He designed a square two-story brick house with seven bedrooms and outbuildings for slaves. He confided to Rachel that he might not live to see their new home finished.

But again, Jackson's country had different plans for him. Before the house was finished, duty called him away from his family. Jackson represented the United States in another treaty-making session with the Choctaws in Mississippi. He opened the meeting by telling the Choctaws that the president knew about their poverty, their economic depression, and their problems with alcohol. He told them that the president wanted to help them. To do so, he would exchange some of the Choctaw land east of the Mississippi for a larger area west of the Mississippi River, "a country of tall trees, many water courses, rich lands and High grass abounding in game of all kinds . . ." A Choctaw chief answered that Jackson knew that the lands he was offering were poor, sterile, and worthless. He and Jackson argued briefly.

Then Jackson shut off the arguments: "If you refuse . . . the nation will be destroyed." The Choctaws capitulated. A press friendly to the government described the treaty as an example of the generosity and kindness of the American government toward their less fortunate neighbors. They praised the administration for their gifts of blankets and kettles to the Indians to help in their re-settlement. Newspapers did not report that there was some opposition from citizens who believed the treaty was a disgrace. The Native Americans left their homelands and traveled west to the wilderness without sufficient food or other supplies.

Among the Americans who protested the inhumane treatment of Native Americans was General Winfield Scott. He ordered his men to provide supplies and to ease the way for the exiles. But his efforts came to little use because of the number of Indians involved and the greed of uncaring whites who rushed to profit from the exodus. Some members in Congress fought against Jackson's attitude toward Native Americans. Their voices were not sufficient to sway their fellow legislators. Some Christian missionaries protested the cruelties and tried to ease the burdens. Except in a few cases where they were arrested for contempt of the law, these missionaries were hardly noticed.

In February 1821, President Monroe again asked Jackson to accept appointment as governor of the Florida territory. Rachel immediately spoke against the move; she had no desire to live in Florida. But Jackson saw an opportunity to rebuild his reputation in an area where he had received a lot of criticism for his military tactics. Added incentive was the salary of $5000, exactly the same as his military salary. On June 1, he retired from the army, and the

Jackson family headed for Florida. Rachel gasped in horror when she first saw New Orleans. She wrote back to her friends: "Oh, the wickedness, the idolatry of the place! Unspeakable the riches and splendor . . . Pray for your sister, in a heathen land, far from my people and church."

On July 17, they arrived in Pensacola followed by American soldiers marching to the strident beat of their band. Governor Cavalla handed Jackson the keys to the city. The Spanish flag was lowered, and the American flag raised. Then they joined in a lavish banquet. But the good will did not prevail. Jackson spoke no Spanish, and Cavalla spoke no English. Through their translators, they argued about who would control the city's cannons and who would have possession of the legal papers and credentials. They argued about who would establish and enforce rules and who would make plans for the future. Jackson argued, but he did not wait for an agreement. He acted quickly to issue ordinances and to proclaim rules and regulations.

In mid-August, Cavalla refused to comply with Jackson's orders to hand over some official papers. Jackson had him put in jail. Then he sent one of his aides to Cavalla's office to get the papers that he wanted. When he had the papers in hand, Jackson released Cavalla. As soon as he was released, Cavalla charged Jackson with false arrest. In a hearing before a judge, Jackson explained calmly that he had a right to do anything necessary to control the government, and that Cavalla had obstructed him. The case was sent to Washington City where Jackson's actions were upheld.

He won the case, but he suffered physical and emotional losses. In October, feeling weak and vulnerable, Jackson told Monroe that he wanted to leave Florida even though he had been there only

General Winfield Scott protested the brutal treatment the Native Americans received during their forced removal to land west of the Mississippi.

eleven weeks. He used the excuse that his wife was ill, and he did not mention his own poor health. He took with him the satisfaction that he had changed Florida in many ways. He had established a wide range of offices including sheriffs and district attorneys to deal with the ever increasing needs of land owners and speculators. He had promoted increased use of the English language. He had insisted on the establishment of democratic procedures in government: Every free white man had the right to vote, all white men were equal under the law, and government could not exceed its bounds except in an emergency. He declared that, once again, he had been a champion of the common man against government domination.

He also left recommendations for dealing with Native Americans: He discouraged making treaties with them. He said that his experiences proved that Native Americans were ignorant, dishonest, and in need of discipline. He told those native people who remained in Florida that white men who lived there would discipline them.

Back at the Hermitage, Jackson was on the verge of collapse. The two bullets lodged in his body caused him pain, and he suffered a myriad of other health problems including chronic respiratory infections with wracking coughs and bleeding from the mouth, dysentery, frequent stomach aches, intermittent fever, and decaying teeth. Among the medications he took were lead and mercury, drugs now known to be poisons. He was also subject to fits of temper and hypersensitivity toward real and imagined criticism.

Family problems made the situation worse. Andrew Jr. did poorly in school and Jackson could not stop him from wasteful spending. Young Andrew Jackson Hutchings, the son of a business partner, had come to live with the Jacksons after his father died.

This Andrew was also a discipline problem, both at home and in school. Jackson loved both boys and supported them loyally, no matter what problems they presented him. Lyncoya, the infant he had adopted, did well in a day school, and Jackson offered to send him to West Point. To his disappointment, the boy preferred to learn the saddler's trade.

Rachel was overjoyed to be back at the Hermitage. For several months, she nursed her husband attentively. Then she returned to management of the house and farm accounts. Her health was poor, perhaps from obesity, perhaps from hypertension. She spent a lot of time practicing her religion, both with a church group and privately. As her husband's health improved, they entertained lavishly in their plantation home. When his health permitted, Jackson was once again a charming host. He was full of jokes, an interesting conversationalist, and a good listener. During a meal, he often walked around the tables, stopping to talk to each guest individually.

During his convalescence, Jackson studied the country's financial conditions. The depression of 1822 had far-ranging consequences, including speculator panic, unemployment, and poor distribution of goods and services. To ease the situation, banks issued paper money. Jackson declared that this currency was worse than worthless since it was not backed by the government. He said that the economy was over-run by fraud all the way from the president down to local bankers. He was proven correct when journalists uncovered scandalous behavior and corruption.

Historians have sometimes called the years 1816-1828 the Era of Corruption. Banks were just one example. Government officials devised many schemes for stealing public monies and for taking bribes in return for favors. Trade with the Native Americans furnished special opportunities for swindles because the native people had no standing in the legal system. The approaching presidential election of 1824 fostered corruption as potential candidates vied with each other to curry favor from big business.

Newspaper articles about the results of Congressional investigations left the American public feeling cheated but unable to correct the problems. They wanted a return to plain and simple government. Andrew Jackson was widely known as a plain and simple man. With increasing fervor, calls came to Jackson asking him to run for president. At first he said, "Do they think I am such a damned fool? I can command a body of men in a rough way, but I am not fit to be President." Still, he did not say no. He said: "I give the same answer that I have never been a candidate for any office. I never will. But the people have a right to chose ... when the people call, the Citizen is bound to render the service required."

The Tennessee House of Representatives unanimously nominated Andrew Jackson for president in July 1822. In the state Senate, a few of Jackson's opponents walked out of the meeting in protest when his name was posed as a possible candidate. The rest of the Senate unanimously and enthusiastically supported him. The senators who had protested decided to go along with the adulation of Old Hickory. They assumed that his fans would soon discover that their hero was merely a frontiersman and military man, obviously incapable of becoming president of the United States. They were wrong. Throughout the country a groundswell for Jackson sounded loud and clear.

One of Jackson's opponents was Senator John Williams of Tennessee. Williams had spread rumors in Washington City that Jackson lacked their state's support. Jackson's supporters retaliated by announcing Old Hickory's run for Senate against encumbent Williams. Although his defeat of Williams would only strengthen his presidential race, Jackson was disappointed. He did not want to spend time in the Senate, which he believed to be corrupt. Rachel echoed his feelings, saying, "I hope he may not be called again to the strife and empty honors of public place." But Old Hickory had two reasons for wanting the seat. One was that he believed it was his duty to his country. The other was that, despite his protestations, he wanted to be president. He ran for senator, and he won.

On December 5, 1822, Andrew Jackson took his seat in the Senate. Tall, straight, with graying hair and military dignity, Old Hickory attracted favorable attention. If his physical problems slowed him down, he would not show it. If he still harbored resentment against those politicians whom he had once criticized, he would not show that either. He attended church, a different one each Sunday. He steered clear of any hint of intrigue or corruption. He scrupulously attended all Senate meetings and recorded his vote on every question. Consistently, he voted for high tariffs against imports to protect the largest manufacturing states like Pennsylvania. He stayed above the arguments of his opponents who criticized his imposition of martial law, his failure to wait for military orders, and his removal of Native Americans. He also shied from any criticism of his likely presidential opponent, John Quincy Adams.

Jackson wrote to Rachel almost daily. He assured her of his love, and he reminded her over and over again that their slaves should be treated humanely, well fed and well clothed and without oppression. He also sent messages to both Andrew Jr. and Lyncoya, telling them to study hard. He said this was especially important to him because he lacked a fine education himself.

After two years in the Senate, Jackson traveled to the Hermitage where he picked up Rachel and some of her family. While still awaiting the presidential returns on December 7, 1824, they arrived in Washington City after twenty-eight days of travel. The family was warmly welcomed in the capitol city. Apparently most people there believed that Jackson would soon be their next president. The electoral vote concerned few citizens. This electoral vote was cast by delegates chosen in each state to elect the president and vice-president. In some states, these electors were chosen by the legislature; in others, a general balloting determined who the electors would be.

By mid-December, all the votes were counted. Jackson had the highest number of popular votes. He was the favorite in every section of the country except New England. But he did not receive the required majority of electoral votes, the votes of delegates chosen to represent the individual states. The Twelfth Amendment to the Constitution dictated that, in cases such as this, the election would be decided by the House of Representatives. Each state would have one vote and would choose among the three highest vote-getters, Jackson, Adams, and Secretary of the Treasury William Crawford. Crawford had run a distant third in the election, and was not considered a contender for president. The contest between Jackson and Adams was tight, and rumors of deal-making, bribery, and conspiracy filled the capital as legislators prepared to cast their votes.

Exhausted by the turmoil, Jackson experienced a bad fall down a flight of stairs. One of the never-healed wounds in his chest broke open. He lay in bed for a week, barely moving, while his body hemorrhaged. Some historians say that he opened his own veins

John Quincy Adams ran against Andrew Jackson in the 1824 presidential election.

with a pen knife trying to mimic bloodletting, a popular medical practice of the times in which a doctor took a pint of blood from his patient, believing that the cause of an illness would drain out with the blood.

As Jackson lay weak and sometimes semi-conscious, the bargaining swirled around the House. On January 24, the Kentucky delegation changed their vote from favorite-son Henry Clay to John Quincy Adams. Political watchers noted that this seemed strange because Adams had not received a single popular vote in that state. In February, the House announced that Adams had won the election. Rumors flew that Adams had made a deal with Henry Clay, who wielded strong influence over the Kentucky delegation. It was suspected that Adams had offered Clay a position in the cabinet if the legislator would swing the vote to Adams.

Jackson shook hands with Adams and congratulated him on the victory, never mentioning the many stories of alleged election fraud. He declared that he would not oppose the duly elected president except when he believed that Adams violated the trust of the American people. Five days after the election, Adams appointed Henry Clay as Secretary of State. Jackson declared that this appointment proved that Adams had violated the trust of the people. Old Hickory asked the public: "Was there ever witnessed such a bare faced corruption in any country before? . . . I shudder for the liberty of my country."

Despite his political defeat and physical repercussions from the fall, Jackson found the strength to adopt a new cause, the need for government reform. He believed that as the hero of the common man and a supporter of democracy, he could lead an effective reform movement. Vice-President Calhoun, a Jackson supporter, agreed to help. Jackson's first action in this new role was to verify, as thoroughly as he could, the cheating and corruption in the recent election. He set up informal headquarters at the Hermitage and entertained a steady stream of visitors, each of whom got an earful about the new reform movement. Many of these visitors pushed him to run for president in the next election. It was obvious that Adams would run again.

In October 1825, the Tennessee legislature nominated Jackson for president.

Chapter Seven

Tie the Bag

When the Tennessee State Legislature nominated Jackson for president, he resigned from the Senate so that he could spend time campaigning. He became the unofficial head of the Democratic Party. He read dozens of newspapers, always with an eye for events and people that he could turn to his advantage. Jackson saw his challenges clearly.

As his country grew, so did big business and government. And as they grew, so did corruption and fraud, reaching to the highest offices of government. Jackson, the champion of the people, promised to rid the country of this fraud. Another challenge lay in removal of Native Americans from land which might be desirable for whites. On the controversial issue of import taxes, Jackson favored high tariffs to protect the manufacturing states from foreign competition. Ever conscious of public opinion, Jackson again rejected Rachel's pleas to join her church. He feared that joining might be seen as currying public favor. He promised to join as soon as the campaign was over.

His determination could not overcome the physical problems that plagued both himself and Rachel. Her health was generally poor, and she was very overweight. Jackson's own health also continued to decline. One rather new problem was his ill-fitting dentures which blurred his speech at times and were a source of constant pain.

He received a big boost in the spring of 1826 from Calhoun. The vice-president, disgusted with what he considered President Adam's mistakes, wrote to Jackson that the country was in danger because of poor administration. He pledged full support for a Jackson-for-president campaign. Less than six months later, Martin Van Buren, an influential politician and candidate for governor of New York, also announced his support of Jackson for president. Van Buren was known in political circles as the "Little Magician" because some said his political skills were so effective they could only be considered magic. Under the leadership of Calhoun and Van Buren, the South and West were essentially united politically for Jackson in the Democratic party.

As Jackson's candidacy looked better and better, opponents stepped up their arguments against him. They claimed that he had lived with Rachel while she was married to another man, and some said that Andrew and Rachel had never been properly married. They called Rachel an adulteress and a bigamist. They reminded the public that Jackson had once allied himself with the traitor Aaron Burr. They brought up the story of Jackson's execution of two British officers in Pensacola and his harsh treatment of Native Americans. They accused him of pretending to support high standards of behavior on one hand and engaging in cockfighting, drinking, and swearing on the other. Other opponents played down the importance of his military victories, saying they had no relevance to his qualifications for the presidency.

Jackson's supporters, calling themselves a Hickory Club, issued pamphlets and reports denying the claims of the opposition as fast as they were announced. They portrayed him as a champion of the people and a believer in democratic principles; they portrayed Adams and his supporters as champions of big business and believers in an elite government. They also manufactured and sold thousands of Jackson souvenirs—badges, beer mugs, plates, and even ladies's combs, with Jackson's picture on them.

On hearing the rumors about their marriage, Rachel, already suffering with heart palpitations and bronchitis, became hysterical. Andrew sympathized with her; he said that all the persecution she suffered made her even dearer to him. In the midst of these family problems, sixteen-year-old Lyncoya died of a respiratory infection. His death was a severe blow to both parents. Rachel lost all her spirit. Jackson recovered enough to manage a strong get-out-the-vote campaign as the 1828 election neared, a campaign decorated with flags and posters and the motto "To the Polls!"

The final tally showed Jackson the winner. He secured 647,000 popular votes, whereas Adams only collected 508,000. Jackson also dominated in the electoral vote, 178 to 83. John Calhoun won the vice-presidency. Jackson, the backwoods frontier hero, had won a smashing victory over the incumbent president. Many saw it as the common people's party winning over the party of the elite. A journalist wrote that the election of Jackson was a victory of democratic principles over the politics of the wealthy.

Rachel did not join the celebrations. She would only say that she was happy for her husband, but she had never wished for his election. While Rachel's friends and relatives excitedly planned a new wardrobe for her, the First-Lady-to-be suffered from depression as well as poor health. "I had rather be a doorkeeper in the house of God than to live in that palace at Washington." Her cold became a serious respiratory infection. As she gasped and writhed for breath in painful spasms, a doctor performed bloodletting. She rallied slightly, then suffered a heart attack. On December 22, 1828, she died.

Andrew's grief was deep. He and Rachel had been together almost forty years. It seemed to him that he might never recover from this tragedy. He said, "My heart is nearly broke." He felt more than sorrow; he also felt anger. He suspected that part of Rachel's health problem was her reaction to the rumors and accusations about their marriage. Jackson vowed revenge on those who had slandered her.

As in other periods of his life, Old Hickory was strengthened by his devotion to duty. His country had called; he could not and would not refuse. He made the three-week trip to Washington by steamboat and then over land in a carriage drawn by two horses. The newly elected president arrived at the capitol in mourning clothes—black suit and tie, white shirt, and black bands on his arm and around his tall beaver hat. He moved into a hotel on February 11 and immediately began a heavy schedule of greeting Congress-men and other government officials as well as job-seekers.

Selecting his cabinet was a priority. Besides considerations of expertise and skill, Jackson kept in mind "payments" to those who had helped him get elected. One of his first appointments was Martin Van Buren as Secretary of State. His advisors shook their heads. To them, Van Buren's nickname of Little Magician spelled trouble. Besides, he had no experience at all in foreign affairs. Jackson also appointed his old friend John Eaton as Secretary of War. Again his advisors shook their heads. They asked how Eaton could participate in government since his wife Margaret had an unseemly reputation. Jackson asked what Eaton's wife would have to do with the duties of the War Department. Advisors answered that neither John nor his wife would be accepted into

Washington social life, and this would be a grave drawback in his political life.

Unaware of this political bickering, thousands of citizens traveled in sulkies, carriages, and on horseback over muddy roads and mere paths to reach the capitol by the time of the inauguration. The taverns, vaudeville shows, and Thomas Jefferson's library were among the most popular sights for tourists. As many guests as possible stayed at Gadsby's Hotel, noted for the half mile of paved road in front of it, the only paved road in the city. Fortunately, the weather was mild, so those who slept under the stars had no great difficulty. On March 4, huge crowds lined the streets to see their hero, the man who would save them from the evils and corruption of big government. They made their way through mud, going around puddles, pigs, and busy slaves to gape at the White House, a simple building with no porticos, pedestals, or columns.

On the morning of the ceremony, fifteen to twenty thousand people moved slowly to the Senate chambers. Jackson appeared in mourning black, a picture of sadness with his gaunt figure and grieving eyes. He sat between Calhoun and Chief Justice John Marshall, the man who would conduct the swearing-in. The chair reserved for John Adams was empty because Adams refused to attend. His refusal was part of a continuing conflict between the two men. Jackson had refused to pay a courtesy call on Adams because he believed that Adams had slandered Rachel. So Adams returned the snub by refusing to appear at the inauguration.

The new president's speech was just ten minutes long. After he spoke, he kissed the Bible held by Chief Justice John Marshall. Then he bowed to the spectators. The crowd roared its approval. The highest officer in the country had bowed to them. He rode a handsome white horse to his new home, and cheering crowds

After Jackson was elected president of the United States, Rachel, his wife of nearly
forty years, died of a heart attack.

followed him. Jackson's plans for a modest reception in the White House were destroyed as hundreds of people swarmed into the house, grabbing barrels of orange punch and smashing glasses. Some stood on the damask chairs, and some on tables, to get a better look at their new president. The floors shook from the weight and movement of so many people. Senator James Hamilton described the scene: "The mob broke in, in thousands . . . poured in one interrupted stream of mud and filth . . ." Margaret Smith, a Washington socialite, said, "Ladies fainted, men were seen with bloody noses and such a scene of confusion . . . But it was the People's day, and the People's president and the People would rule . . ."

Around 4:00, a group of men formed a ring around the new president, shielding him from the swarming crowds to keep him from being injured in the crush. With their help, Jackson escaped to the peace and quiet of his hotel. Staff at the White House moved the food and drink outside, a successful plan to get the crowds out of the building. The President's Ball that evening was an elegant affair, attended only by the 1200 people who were specifically invited. Tickets were five dollars, too much for the common person. Jackson did not attend since he was still in mourning.

In hindsight, the day was declared a success by both spectators and reporters. The noisy participation by citizens was a sign that this was, indeed, a new kind of presidency, one that focused on common people. With a Congressional grant of $50,000 Jackson renovated the White House, undoing the damage done during the inauguration. He added some touches of his own such as the twenty new spittoons in the East Room. Jackson's son Andrew and some of Rachel's relatives moved into the White House.

Jackson became president at a time when many issues that had been stewing for years seemed to come to a boil. He was determined to correct the things he saw as wrongs or injustices in the federal government. He was no more afraid to stand up to his enemies in Washington than he had been in Tennessee.

One of the new president's first actions was to establish a "rotation" plan, under which government workers were limited to a four-year term to prevent them from abusing their position. He discovered that over $280,000 had been stolen from the Treasury department and he indicted eleven Treasury agents. He fired dozens of other workers found guilty of stealing in other departments. In his first year, expenses of the Navy Department decreased by $1 million as a result of Jackson's discovery of embezzlement.

The other side of the story involved Jackson's replacements. Job seekers walked into the White House freely, asking for jobs and often speaking directly to the president. There were approximately 500 applicants for every open position. Jackson soon found out that it was extremely difficult to select the best candidates. His attempts to reform government workers were no more successful than those of presidents who served before him.

Serious family problems added to the strains of the job. He still mourned for Rachel. Living with his in-laws posed daily problems. Andrew Jackson, Jr. was involved in romantic entanglements that his father disapproved of. His ward Andrew Jackson Hutchings could not or would not study or behave appropriately. Jackson worried because he heard rumors that his overseer at the Hermitage was inhumane toward his slaves.

The new president became seriously involved in rumors of scandal again. Gossip continued to swirl around Margaret Eaton, and this gossip hurt her husband's effectiveness as Secretary of

War. It was said that Mrs. Eaton had led a life of immoral behavior since girlhood, and therefore, neither she nor her husband were accepted socially. Jackson remained loyal to both John and Margaret. He sent investigators to disprove the accusations against Mrs. Eaton. He openly quarreled with a highly respected minister who insisted that Mrs. Eaton was, indeed, a sinner. Jackson said, "Female virtue is like a tender and delicate flower, let but the breath of suspicion rest upon it, and it withers and perhaps perishes forever."

He would not let the matter drop. He called a cabinet meeting of all officers except Eaton, and he issued an ultimatum. He said that he would not remove Eaton from the cabinet and that any members who disapproved or disagreed were free to leave their newly appointed positions. That ultimatum quieted but did not end the so-called Petticoat War. He had won the battle, but the emotional conflict left scars. Listening to the criticisms of Margaret Eaton brought back the agonies he and Rachel had suffered over the same kind of scandal. Perhaps the emotional distress caused physical discomfort. His feet and legs swelled, and he felt generally weak, a problem he called "dropsy." Some of those nearest to him wondered if he would succumb to these health problems.

Despite all his difficulties, Old Hickory kept the government running. He met regularly and knowledgeably with department officials, delegated authority, supported his staff, and kept careful watch over all expenditures. He continued his quest to include Texas as a state, even offering $5 million to Mexico for this territory. The economy was strong, and he had hopes of paying down the $48.5 million federal debt.

In his December 1829 state of the union address to Congress, Jackson declared that he was grateful to God for all the good his

Jackson's advisors had warned the president about naming controversial John Eaton as Secretary of War.

government had done for its twenty-four states and 12 million people. He mentioned specifically his satisfaction that the national debt was reduced, and he expected to see it drop even lower during his term of office. He supported states' rights saying that most of the laws of the country should be written in state legislatures, not in the Congress.

He battled with Congress over what he considered unnecessary spending. Legislators piled appropriation bills on Jackson's desk, asking for federal money for items such as dredging harbors, building lighthouses, and purchasing stock in a canal company. Jackson vetoed most of them, arguing: "I was elected to pay off the national debt. How can I do that and pay for these improvements without borrowing? It cannot be done—and borrow I will not."

Conflict grew between the North and South over import tariff bills. Representatives of industrial northern states favored high import taxes. These fees restricted competition by raising the prices on goods made in foreign countries. This way they were able to charge more for their goods, insuring profits and growth. The northern representaives said that it was good for the entire country to have a strong manufacturing base.

Representatives of southern states favored lower taxes to allow cheaper goods to come into the country. Few southerners were engaged in manufacturing. They were mostly farmers, and many wanted to sell their crops overseas. But the European countries raised their tariffs on American crops to retaliate for the American tariffs on their manufactured goods. This cut into the profits of cotton, tobacco, and other crops grown in the South. So southern farmers were hurt two ways by the tarriff: It cut into their sales of crops and raised the prices of the goods they had to buy from merchants.

To many in the South, high tariffs were just another example of what they saw as the growing northern domination of national politics. A group of southern leaders, led by Vice-President Calhoun, devised a theory they called nullification. This theory said that because the national government had been formed by a voluntary agreement of the states, the states were the ultimate final authority of which acts that the U.S. Congress passed were consitutional. They argued that a state could hold a convention and vote to declare a national law as null and void because it violated the Constitution.

Although he was from an area of the nation that generally supported lower tariffs, Jackson supported a tariff. He did agree to ask for some lower penalties to relax the burden. The president, however, was strongly opposed to nullification. Jackson left no doubt about his stand. At a Jefferson Day Dinner, attended by Calhoun and other supporters of nullification, Jackson rose and made a toast that became famous. Many of the attendees had spoken before him passionately for states' rights and nullification. Jackson stood and announced simply: "Our Federal Union: It must be preserved!"

In South Carolina, supporters of nullification called for a volunteer militia to enforce their decision to secede. Thousands of Carolinians wore replicas of palmetto trees and buttons with the slogan, "John Calhoun, First President of the Southern Confederacy." Jackson ordered officers and troops to be on the alert in the Charleston area. He issued a proclamation to the people of South Carolina, declaring that no state could secede, and that state officials who advocated secession were also advocating treason. In Congress, a southern representative shrieked and stamped, declaring "South Carolina is oppressed. Yes, sir, a tyrant majority sucks her life blood from her."

Jackson answered calmly that, if he had to, he could have two thousand men ready to march south, and in less than two months, they would squash completely any insurrection. He went on: "If this thing [secession] goes on, our country will be like a bag of meal with both ends open. Pick it up in the middle or endwise, and it will run out. I must tie the bag and save the country." Calhoun encouraged secession: "The hope of the country now rests on our gallant little State. Let every Carolinian do his duty."

Eventually, Jackson reached a compromise. If the nullifiers would drop the idea of secession the tariff would be lowered. Jackson spearheaded the compromise with two bills. In the Compromise Tariff Bill, he proposed that tariff rates be reduced by half. In the Force Bill, he declared that the Union could never be broken up in any way. This bill authorized him to use militia if necessary to put down secession. Both bills passed. President Jackson, whom many had called a hothead, had shown that he could use diplomacy as a tool of his presidency.

Chapter Eight

I Will Kill It

President Jackson sent generals to the Cherokees and Creeks to persuade the Native Americans to voluntarily move to land across the Mississippi River. He asked Chickasaw and Choctaw leaders to sign treaties and to agree to obey the removal bill passed by Congress. The Choctaws refused to come to the treaty signing. Jackson opened the meeting with the Chickasaws by saying, "To these laws, where you are, you must submit;—there is no preventive—no other alternative. Your great father cannot, nor can congress, prevent it . . . Old men! Lead your children to a land of promise and of peace before the Great Spirit shall call you to die. Young chiefs! Preserve your people and nation . . ." The Chickasaws answered that they were ready to accept a treaty based on the principles outlined to them. The meeting ended with affectionate farewells on both sides. One chief held out his hands to Jackson and said, "God bless you, my great father."

In the fall of 1830, Jackson had big plans for his administration. He hoped to pay off the national debt by 1833. He increased the power of the presidency by vetoing more legislation than all previous presidents together. He believed that he had restored virtue to the American government. He planned to improve relations with Great Britain, especially with regard to trade. He planned to smooth relations with France concerning the many conflicts relating to the Louisiana treaty.

There was no doubt about it—Jackson wanted another term in office. There was also no doubt that he had to overcome severe criticism from both major parties about his unfortunate cabinet choices. Little Magician Van Buren came up with a solution to that problem. He told Jackson that he would resign from his cabinet position, and John Eaton would do the same. With these important resignations, Jackson could justify a reorganization of the whole cabinet. In April 1831, Van Buren, Eaton, and two other members resigned. Jackson announced that he would appoint a whole new cabinet.

Those changes did not quiet Jackson's opposition. Some opponents hit upon the catchy phrases "Parlor Cabinet" and "Kitchen Cabinet" to imply that Jackson paid less attention to his appointed advisors (the Parlor Cabinet) and more attention to intimate friends (the Kitchen Cabinet). Other opponents, including some Democrats, suggested that Jackson's poor health might prevent him from serving another term. Calhoun, in support of his own bid for the presidency, published a fifty-page report in which he criticized Jackson's role in the conflict against the Seminoles. Opponents asked how a president who claimed to be a symbol for individual freedom could support removal of Native Americans. Some opponents criticized the president severely because he refused to designate a day of prayer when a cholera epidemic swept the country.

Jackson had answers for all the criticisms. He had a new cabinet, so no one could fault him on that score. He said that Calhoun was the "most profound hypocrite he had ever known" and a danger to the country. He insisted that his treatment of Native Americans was not only humane, but kind, the actions of a responsible father toward his little children. He justified his decision not to designate a day of prayer by saying that it would interfere with the separation of church and state.

Another problem in Jackson's candidacy swirled around the Bank of the United States (BUS), which called itself the National Bank. This was not a national bank; it was a privately controlled banking corporation with profitable ties to the federal government. Wealthy stockholders of the bank had three advantages. The government deposited money in the bank, and the bank paid no interest on the deposits. The bank paid no taxes in the state of Pennsylvania where it did business. Furthermore, by law, Congress could not charter any institution which would compete with the BUS. Jackson said that these government-sponsored advantages worked against the democratic principles he had established for the country. Nicholas Biddell, president of the BUS, and his stockholders insisted that the bank played a significant role in the economic health of the country.

The conflict continued, adding to a particularly difficult summer for Jackson. He was lonely. He frequently wept at Rachel's grave in the garden at the Hermitage, praying, "I only wish if it pleased the will of providence, that I was by her side, free from all the deception and depravity of this wicked world." His headaches were almost constant, and he was afflicted with general physical weakness. He did have a streak of good luck when a surgeon suggested that he could remove the bullet from Jackson's arm. The president rolled up his sleeve and ordered him to begin. The surgeon made the incision and squeezed Jackson's arm. The bullet fell to the floor. The operation seemed to be a success. Later that night, Jackson was able to attend a dinner party. A few other bright spots in his personal life included Andrew Jr.'s engagement and the promise from Andrew Jackson Hutchings that he would be an industrious student at the University of Virginia.

In January 1832, BUS president Biddle petitioned Congress to re-charter the bank. Jackson believed that the BUS had made extensive, politically motivated loans to both newspapermen and to Congressmen. When Congress passed the bill, Jackson vetoed it. "The bank . . . is trying to kill me, *but I will kill it!*" he said. He added that it was deplorable that rich and powerful people used the government to meet selfish goals.

The veto delighted Biddle who was sure that both Congress and the American people would turn against Jackson. Biddle was wrong. The veto brought even more support to the president who had told citizens that he was fighting against the greedy rich for the rights of poor people.

Jackson achieved more with the federal economy than he did with his own finances. By the beginning of 1832, he was in debt. His salary of $25,000 did not cover his extensive entertaining. He had spent lavishly on his son's marriage. His personal and family problems multiplied. Hutchings was expelled from college for absenteeism. The president caught the flu, and this kept him down for several weeks. Coughing and heavy smoking caused abscesses in his lungs to flare up, creating pain, infection, and bleeding.

Politically, Jackson also experienced problems. He had nominated Van Buren as minister to Great Britain. When the vote on the nomination ended in a tie in the Senate, Calhoun broke the tie with a vote against the Little Magician. Jackson was so angry that he asked Van Buren to be his running mate in the coming election. Van Buren accepted.

Vice-President John C. Calhoun disagreed with Jackson over nullification and state's rights.

Old Hickory began a strong campaign. He forced himself to appear in public more often. He was never too busy to shake hands, share greetings, or listen to pleas. Some of his advisors warned him that he would wear himself out with all this socializing. Jackson insisted that the White House was the People's House, and the only way they could recognize that was to be treated like guests there. He added two wings to the White House to accommodate Andrew Jr. and his pregnant wife, created a dining room that could seat a hundred guests, added porticos in front and back, and painted and re-papered the whole house.

Ever mindful that this country was a people's democracy, Jackson proposed a change in the process of nominating national candidates in the Democratic party. In place of the present state and local conventions dominated by political bosses, Jackson proposed a national convention attended by delegates elected by the people. Supporters of Jackson eagerly accepted this proposal. The first national Democratic nominating convention opened in May of 1832 in Baltimore, Maryland. They adopted a unit rule by which the majority of each delegation cast the entire vote for the state. Obviously Jackson was their presidential candidate. Van Buren received the vote for vice-president. The Republicans nominated Henry Clay for president and John Sergeant of Pennsylvania for vice-president.

Jackson's supporters showered the public with pamphlets, newspapers, barbecues, and parades, some as long as a mile. Citizens loved these parades with their focus on Jackson as a backwoodsman, soldier, a common citizen immune to the glamor of wealth and social status. The Jackson Presidency stood for equality of opportunity for all white males. Fifteen million Americans were defining themselves as a new people, unlike their

European ancestors in many ways. They were particularly eager to explore, to accept challenges, and to work. They expanded the country with canals, railroads, turnpikes, roads. The arts flourished with writers like Ralph Waldo Emerson and Nathaniel Hawthorne and artists like John James Audubon and Gilbert Stuart. They were eager to welcome the informal democratic style that Jackson brought to the presidency. Jackson was re-elected with about 150,000 more popular votes than Clay and with 170 more electoral votes.

On Inauguration Day, Jackson held his slender body—6 feet tall, 140 pounds—with military stiffness. His long full coat and tall beaver hat added to his dignity. Still, many spectators remarked that he looked emaciated, even feeble. The temperature was only 11 degrees Fahrenheit and snow covered the ground. He shivered, gave his speech, and went home to bed. He was unable to attend the inaugural balls held that night because he was exhausted.

But there was no rest in sight for the newly re-elected president. Jackson believed he could pay off the national debt by using $6 million of government bonds being held in the Bank of the United States. He asked to withdraw those funds. Biddle told him that the withdrawal would have a bad effect on the economy. Jackson insisted on getting the money. Biddle stalled, and Jackson began an investigation of bank operations.

On the personal side, Jackson found the deteriorating financial situation at the Hermitage a constant worry. His health problems— weakness, pain, and indigestion—left him more fragile than ever. His doctor no longer prescribed the bloodletting. He feared that Jackson could not withstand losing the prescribed pint of blood. At one low point for Jackson, the doctor prescribed a plaster of dried beetles on his chest. Jackson recovered, and no one will ever know if the recovery was due to the beetles or to the patient's invincible spirit.

By January, Biddle admitted that the government funds were not in the bank; they had been used for investment by the bank officers. This was a flagrant violation of the contract between the bank and the government. That was the last straw for Old Hickory. He resolved to destroy the BUS. His advisors agreed with him that the bank had to go, but they urged him to wait until other banks could take over the functions of the BUS. Jackson set a deadline of September. By that time, he wanted state banks to be ready to accept all government deposits.

In May 1833, President Jackson was traveling in a steamboat to Fredericksburg, Virginia. A fellow traveler named Robert Randolph approached the president, seeming to want to shake Jackson's hand. Instead of grasping his hand, Randolph hit him. Blood spurted from Jackson's face.

Jackson tried to rise to defend himself but could not move because he was wedged behind a table. The president's attendants grabbed Randolph before he could hit again. They asked Jackson if he wanted them to kill Randolph. Jackson shook his bleeding head. He said that he would have taken care of the man himself if only he could have moved more quickly. But since he could not beat the man himself, he wanted him arrested and punished for his crime.

Chapter Nine

The Majority Is to Govern

The bruise on Jackson's face left from the attack on the steamboat soon healed and left no lasting damage. He played the scene in his mind over and over. The more he thought about it, the more he suspected that the attack was part of a political plot against him. His suspicions were confirmed when he learned that Randolph pleaded guilty only to the act of pulling Jackson's nose at his trial. The judge declared that this was not a criminal act, and Randolph was freed. Jackson admitted to himself that he could no longer be fearless. He continued to travel but now protected himself with a military guard.

One of his tours was a trip around New England, New York, and Pennsylvania with the goal of building support for Democrats. Although Northerners generally favored those opposed to Jackson's party, they greeted President Jackson with bands, parades, banquets, speeches, and mobs. Jackson created an aura of popularity, charisma, and enthusiasm unlike the more formal presidents who preceded him.

On his itinerary was a trip to Harvard College in Massachusetts to receive an honorary Doctor of Laws degree. John Quincy Adams blasted Harvard for awarding him this honor. He asked how the prestigious college could honor a "a barbarian who could not write a sentence of grammar and hardly could spell his own name." Some of Jackson's critics created mock scenarios in which Old Hickory made a fool of himself accepting the degree. They cartooned him as completely confused over the use of sophisticated English. They showed him as even more confused by the use of Latin. Once again, Jackson's critics had underestimated him. At the ceremony and a reception afterwards, Old Hickory was a model of sophistication and charm.

But also, once again, Jackson's health suffered under the strain of public celebrations. As he traveled on to other Massachusetts towns, he became more feeble, and had to take frequent naps. He no longer tried to hide his poor health from his fans. At one stop when he invited a supporter to visit him at the White House, he added that he hoped he would live to return to Washington City himself. Finally he knew he could not follow the travel schedule planned for him. He returned to Washington City with his feet and ankles so swollen that he could stand only with difficulty. He began a schedule of regular fasting, horseback riding as exercise, and doses of the laxative calomel. Jackson prayed often and went to church every Sunday.

As he gradually improved, he returned to the BUS question. He believed that he had been patient long enough. He suggested to Secretary of the Treasury William Duane that they insist the BUS outline a plan to pay back all deposits. If the bank officers did not agree, Jackson would remove all government deposits at once. Duane opposed the idea. Jackson's mind was made up, and he would not let Duane stand in his way. The president asked Duane to resign from the Treasury Department in return for an appointment as ambassador to Russia. Duane seemed to agree. But as soon as Jackson made the public announcement about the funds, Duane said that he would not resign. Jackson's response was immediate—he said he would fire Duane.

Before this question was resolved, Biddle planned to create an economic crisis that would force Jackson to re-charter the BUS. He threatened to raise interest rates and to call in all loans to state banks. As Biddell hoped, businessmen went to Jackson and begged him to re-charter the bank. Jackson answered these men: "Go to Nicholas Biddell. Biddle has all the money…Andrew Jackson will never re-charter that monster of corruption!" Harsh criticism of Jackson exploded throughout the country. Justice Joseph Story of the Supreme Court said, "Though we live under the form of a republic, we are in fact under the absolute rule of a single man." Another judge said, "I look upon Jackson as a detestable, ignorant, reckless, vain & malignant tyrant."

As he had threatened, Jackson fired Duane. Then he ordered that all government deposits be removed from the BUS. He pushed through approval of twenty-two state banks to hold government funds. Up to this point, it seemed that Jackson's plan was working. But Biddle also had a plan, and his plan was to force re-chartering by making the BUS indispensable to business. He raised interest on loans and indicated that this interest rate would drop if and when the BUS were re-chartered. He refused to grant new loans to businesses until the bank was re-chartered. Squeezed for credit, businessmen again appealed to Jackson to support an extension of the charter for the bank.

Jackson refused. He said that the conflict between the BUS and the U. S. government was an example of the never-ending struggle of wealthy schemers against honest working people. Biddle also remained firm. He said, "My own course is decided.

All other Banks and all the merchants may break, but the Bank of the United States shall not break."

With the BUS conflict at a stand-off, Jackson continued to work on other aspects of finance. People working with small transactions were often stymied by the money supply since paper money came only in large denominations, and small denomination coins were very scarce. To force banks to put more coins in circulation, Jackson proposed a regulation to prohibit banks from issuing paper money in denominations under five dollars. This would force them to keep increasingly larger stocks of coins on hand and to get them into circulation. After the use of coins became more widespread, he planned to prevent banks from issuing notes under twenty dollars, and this would further accelerate the use of coins. Thus, the laboring classes would have money available in amounts that served their purposes. The idea was too innovative for some people and incomprehensible to others. Even some Democrats opposed it.

Still, Jackson wrote his annual speech to Congress with some confidence in the way he had handled the highest office in the land. He singled out a few successes. The national debt was reduced to less than $5 million. The BUS was no longer an enemy of the working people. He bragged about his Native American program that had removed from the American mainstream those people who, he said, did not have the intelligence, morality, or work habits of the rest of the county.

Henry Clay used that speech as a basis on which to attack Jackson's programs, style, and attitudes. He rose in Congress to shout "We are in the midst of a revolution, hitherto bloodless, but rapidly tending towards a total change of the pure republican character of the Government."

Henry Clay's outspoken opposition to many of Jackson's reforms culminated in the senate when he recommended the first presidential censure in American history.

Clay asked Congress to record a censure, an official disapproval, against Jackson. The president's immediate reaction was rage. But on second thought, he decided that perhaps Clay was right. Perhaps Jackson was instigating a revolution, and this is exactly what he had promised when he was a candidate. He had indeed created a revolution in political thought with his insistence that presidents wielded power because they were the voice of the people who elected them. His "revolution" was a victory for the middle and lower classes and a defeat for the rich. The slogan which he repeated so often—"The majority is to govern"—was a fundamentally revolutionary idea.

While Congress debated the censure, Jackson met with John Ross, the chief of the Cherokee Nation. Ross demanded that the Cherokees be allowed to retain some of the land of their ancestors in the southern states. Jackson refused, saying the Cherokees had no right to any land east of the Mississippi. Then Ross demanded $20 million because the United States had broken treaties it made with the Cherokee nation. Jackson refused again, saying the treaties were invalid because the United States had never recognized the Cherokee nation. Ross then asked the president to leave the questions up to the Senate. Jackson agreed. The Senate voted and Jackson's demands were upheld by just one vote.

The Senate, under Clay, moved steadily toward a resolution of censure against Jackson. The motion to censure charged that Jackson had over-reached his executive power when he removed government money from the BUS. On March 28, 1834, the motion to censure Jackson passed by 26 to 20. This was the first time in American history that a president was censured.

Immediately, Jackson published a full report of his actions on the BUS problem. He declared that he was the elected represen-

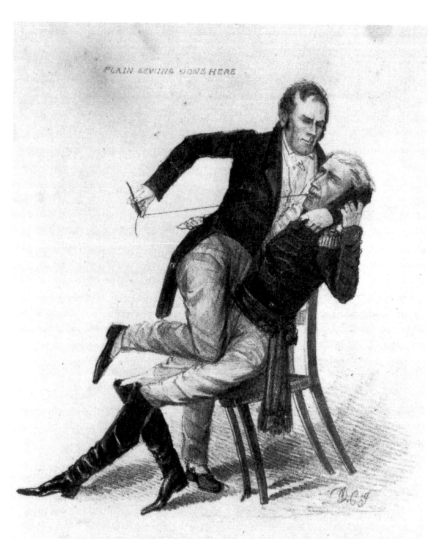

SYMPTOMS' OF A LOCKED JAW

Newspapers raced to parody Henry Clay's movement to censure President Jackson. In this illustration, Clay is attempting to sew Jackson's mouth shut.

Andrew Jackson

tative of the American people, and it was his duty to protect them from the kind of fraud perpetrated by the BUS. Emotions and opinions resounded throughout the country. Supporters admired his stand, calling him a great democrat. Opponents criticized him, calling him an unconstitutional, power-hungry leader. One political party benefitted from this confusion. This was the Whigs, named for the party in Britain which opposed the king. American Whigs said they also opposed a king, "King Andrew." They said they supported government action by legislative mandate not by executive order.

America was expanding rapidly. Geographically, the frontier moved westward. Economically, new businesses and markets developed to meet the increasing population. Politically, Jackson's definition of a democracy was highly controversial, the government's first attempt to speak to the common man.

Even in his weak physical condition, Jackson caught the contagious excitement. He was able to work around his physical problems, but Old Hickory could not sidestep the emotional turmoil in his family. His son, daughter-in-law, and favorite grand-daughter, Rachel, had returned to Tennessee. Jackson was desolate. He missed the company of his son and the family atmosphere created by his daughter-in-law. He particularly missed little Rachel. Andrew Jr. was a special worry. He spent recklessly on the Hermitage. He was unwilling or unable to follow his father's often repeated advice not to buy anything on credit that was not absolutely necessary.

At the White House, Jackson Sr. did not follow his own advice. He was a spendthrift in many ways. His receptions and dinner parties were elegant, well-attended, frequent, and very expensive. He ordered a 440-piece set of French china, a 412-piece dessert set, new cooking utensils, and new furniture. Under a thirty-two candle chandelier, he served French soup, wild turkey, fish, chicken, canvasback ducks, partridges, pheasants, and ham—all at the same meal. Desserts featured tarts, puddings, dried fruits, ice cream, and fruits. President Jackson was renowned for the variety in his wine cellar. He kept to his diet of bread and vegetables, but he made sure that his guests were fed lavishly, perhaps too lavishly. When Jackson added up the bills, he found that his annual hospitality expenses surpassed his annual $25,000 salary.

Included in these expenses were frequent open houses to which the public was invited. At some of these gatherings, mobs crowded into the White House. At one memorable party, a delegation from New York State presented the president with a 1400-pound cheese, four feet around and two feet thick. Old Hickory left it in a place of honor in the White House vestibule to cure for almost two years. After it had cured, he extended an invitation to anyone who wanted to come to enjoy the cheese. A reporter wrote that the air smelled of cheese for half a mile around the White House. Leaving some on the rugs and furniture, the mob finished it off in about two hours.

Social events at the White House were the talk of the town. Some of the wealthy guests sneered at the dress and manners of middle- and lower-class guests. They spread rumors that some visitors were so eager for refreshments that they rushed at the serving butlers. The butlers reportedly armed themselves with sticks to insure safe passage through the grasping crowds.

Jackson's financial situation suddenly became worse when the Hermitage burned, almost to the ground. Sparks from a chimney had probably ignited the roof, and the fire spread quickly in a strong northwest wind. Andrew Jr. blamed the servants: "The cursed negroes were all so stupid & confused that nothing could be done until some white one came to their relief." Andrew Sr. accepted the fire as an accident. He said that the Lord's will had been done.

After losing the Hermitage, Jackson's life was threatened again by another attacker. Jackson was leaving a funeral when he faced a would-be assassin. Thirty-year-old Richard Lawrence stood less than three feet from the president, drew a pistol, and aimed at Jackson's heart. The pistol misfired twice, probably due to the exceptionally humid atmosphere. Jackson rushed at Lawrence with his walking cane raised. Before Jackson could reach him, his aides had wrestled Lawrence to the ground. Jackson tried to club him with his cane as he lay there. Officials pulled Jackson away, hustled him into a carriage, and sped to the White House. Jackson suspected that Lawrence was part of a plot to kill him, but no proof was found. At a trial, he was found not guilty on grounds of insanity and sent to an asylum.

As Old Hickory was recovering from the attack, news about the federal money system helped raise his spirits. Congress passed a Coinage Act authorizing the minting and distribution of gold and silver coins. Because of the president's pressure for such an act, the coins were known as "Jackson money." Also, support for the BUS became so weak that Congress passed a resolution against re-chartering. Today, economists pose questions about the results of Jackson's plan to spread government deposits around in state banks. Some say that the plan set the United States banking system on a firm foundation. Others say that the severe economic down-turn that began soon after the BUS died was a direct result of changes in the system.

The end of his worries about the money system did not bring

Andrew Jackson Jr. was the head of household when the Hermitage burned to the ground.

respite to Jackson. He was not satisfied with the progress of removal of Native Americans. He told the Seminoles that he was disappointed with them because they had not moved west as ordered. "You have no right to stay," he said, "and you must go." When Seminole Chief Oscala threatened retaliation, Jackson had the chief jailed. Jackson had hoped after his jail term Oscala would be subdued. The opposite happened. Oscala rushed back to his tribe with an even more intense hatred of white men. Battle after battle followed; sometimes the whites were victorious, sometimes the Seminoles. Battlegrounds filled with wounded and dead on both sides.

Chapter Ten

We Will Meet in Heaven

Despite Jackson's successes, other domestic problems increased due to many of his reforms. As American industry, transportation, westward migration, and prosperity grew, so did urban crime and violence, materialism, and class bigotry. Slavery became more important to southern farmers, and disputes flared throughout America. In Congress, Jackson's opponents yelled, screamed, and pounded their fists to make their points against Jackson and his administration. Abolitionists, people opposed to slavery, blamed the president for not banning slave trade. Anti-abolitionists blamed him for not putting down the abolition movement which threatened the country. The House passed a resolution declaring that interference with slavery was unconstitutional and that all mention of abolition be forbidden in Congress. This gag rule, known as the Pinckney resolution in honor of a strong supporter, created conflict in Congress for many years.

One specific domestic problem that Jackson faced squarely was poor mail service and increasing debt in the United States Postal Service. Jackson appointed a new postmaster general, and reform began immediately. The new standards created for management became a model for other government departments. The efficiency reinforced Jackson's reputation as a reformer.

Next, a $5 million international issue demanded Jackson's attention. In 1831, the French had agreed to pay damages for American shipping losses incurred when the French seized American ships during the Napoleonic wars. By the end of 1834, they had made no payment on the debt. Jackson demanded immediate payment and threatened reprisal if his demand was not met. The French government took offense at the threat and ordered its ambassador to the United States to return to France. One report said a French official returned the threat with one of his own: "The long sword of France can reach far." Americans reacted in the same spirit of defiance. Hundreds offered to serve in the military against the French. They offered and then could only wait. The French were not quick to reply, and communication across the Atlantic was slow.

On May 26, the news came that the French deputies had passed an indemnity bill, a promise to compensate for damages. But there was a catch. In return for payment, Americans would have to apologize to the French for their threats. Jackson announced that there would be no apology. England offered to mediate the conflict, and Jackson accepted. The case was settled with no apology from Jackson and with indemnity payment from France.

In May 1836, the Senate voted on the New Echota Treaty in which the American government repeated Jackson's demands for removal of Native Americans. It included provisions for reimbursement of $5 million to be split among those Indians who accepted the removal. To enforce the treaty, militia were sent into Cherokee country armed with rifles and bayonets. They seized men, women, and children and burned their homes. They herded them into stockades from which they were sent in groups of a thousand or so on their way west. About 18,000 Cherokees were forcibly removed; about 4000 of them died as a result either of the severe conditions of detention or the 800-mile trip. Removal of the Creeks was just as brutal. Over 10,000 federal troops were enlisted to push them west. After many bloody skirmishes, tortures, and killings, most of the Creeks moved west.

Jackson felt some satisfaction, but he knew that removal was not yet complete. He also knew that he could not endure the rigors of another term in office. But he could not, or would not, let his reform stop at the end of his term. He was determined that Van Buren should succeed him to carry on his programs. He was optimistic when 600 delegates unanimously nominated Van Buren for president at the Democratic national convention in 1836.

With an eye to helping Van Buren's candidacy, Jackson watched Congress. Legislators were debating the use of over $20 million in surplus funds. Jackson wanted the money spent on public works like education and roads. Most legislators, looking ahead to the next election, wanted to please their constituencies by returning the surplus directly to state governments. Jackson weighed his desire to help the country against his desire to please the legislators who would be influential in the coming election. He chose to please the legislators, hoping they would transfer their approval of his actions to approval of Vice-President Van Buren.

Satisfied with this decision, Jackson retreated to the Rip Raps, a government-owned resort on the Potomac. He hoped that rest and recuperation would help to ease his physical problems: Constant pain in his side, swollen feet, and a continual hacking cough. He found no rest there because of the news that street riots had erupted in Charleston, South Carolina. The conflict was over slavery and the right of citizens to send anti-slavery material through the federal mail. Gangs burst into the post office, grabbed incoming mail, and set it on fire. After that incident, a delegation of South Carolina officials met every mailboat coming into the harbor, determined to burn any materials they thought might incite anti-slavery action. Jackson stood on both sides of the issue. He supported the national law which forbade destruction of mail. However, he declared that local officials would have the last word in any given case. This evasive answer avoided a potentially explosive criticism of him in Congress.

In Washington City too, riots erupted over distribution of anti-slavery material. Public demonstrations led to personal injuries and destruction of property. Jackson was not evasive in this situation. He called out U.S. troops to guard public buildings. The immediate result was a slow-down, but not an end to the demonstrations. Whig leaders said that Jackson was responsible for the riots because he had given political power to the masses. They declared that Jackson had created Mobocracy, not democracy. They said that abolitionists were trying to destroy the government. Jackson did not believe that abolitionists could have that much power. He said, "I have great confidence in the virtue of the great majority of the people." The riots continued; the abolitionist movement continued to spread.

Jackson's final open house in the White House brought a huge crowd, all of whom wanted to shake the president's hand and to thank him for his service. A committee from New York presented him with a handsome carriage. Other gifts arrived at the White House from people in all walks of life.

During the last session of Congress under Jackson, Democrats tried to delete from their record the censure of their hero. The Whigs were just as eager to keep the censure as the Democrats were to get rid of it. The vote on censure was taken after thirteen hours of debate. Twenty-four senators voted to delete it; nineteen voted to retain it. The censure was ringed in black and officially deleted from the minutes.

Jackson left for the newly-rebuilt Hermitage in July. The mansion, renovated in the Greek revival style, was more elegant than the old one. Six columns supported a portico, two additional wings added about forty feet to the original measurements of the house, and the double porch extended ten feet forward. Inside, a large central hallway ran the entire length of the building leading to a magnificent flowing staircase that led to the second floor.

The beauty of the Hermitage and the peaceful life there did not isolate Jackson from politics. One matter he wanted settled before he left office was the acquisition of Texas. Americans were settling there in increasing numbers, and Jackson felt encouraged that this would someday be United States territory. But the American-Mexican border had not been officially established, and both Mexico and the United States claimed the territory. When Jackson heard that Mexican authorities in Texas were harassing the American consul, he threatened retaliation "if they touch the hair of the head of one of our citizens, tell him [the consul] to batter down & destroy their town & exterminate the inhabitants from the face of the earth!"

In November 1836, Old Hickory coughed so hard that he hemorrhaged. Relatives, servants, and friends feared for his life as he lay semiconscious for several days. Then he began to recover, but very slowly. For weeks, he was listless, without strength. He suffered from shortness of breath, poor digestion, chronic pain in his side, and spells of coughing. While those around him worried about his health, Jackson worried only about his ability to write his final State of the Union message. (During the nineteenth century, presidents did not give a State of the Union speech, but submitted a written copy to Congress.) He was cheered by Van Buren's victory in the 1836 election.

As Jackson looked back at his tenure, he felt proud. He had moved about 46,000 Native Americans beyond the Mississippi River. The United States had acquired about 100 million acres of land in the East in return for 32 million acres in the West. The economy had grown, and many citizens had prospered. He had maintained a fight against fraud and inefficiency in government. He had destroyed a bank he believed to be corrupt. He had expanded markets among the states and abroad. Most importantly, he had established a new presidential style as a leader who was accessible to the masses. He ended his message by thanking Americans for their support and then predicting his death: "My own race is nearly run; advanced age and failing health warn me that before long I must pass beyond the reach of human events."

Around 11:30 on March 4, 1837, Jackson relaxed with a few close friends after delivering his farewell speech. He drank a glass of wine. As the chimes on the clock struck twelve, he said "Gentlemen, I am no longer President of the United States... I am very glad to get away from all this excitement and bother."

The next day, Jackson escorted Van Buren to the Capitol where the new president gave an hour-long address. After the ceremony, the crowd roared wildly for Jackson as the former president made his way down the steps toward his waiting carriage.

He was out of office but far from free of trouble. Because of Andrew Jr.'s poor management, debts from the Hermitage were over $15,000, and there seemed to be no way of paying them. Jackson had returned from the White House with just ninety dollars

Andrew Jackson was the first president to be photographed.

in his pocket. His cattle were in poor condition, grain had not been stored for them, and his house needed repairs.

His family gave him some comfort, especially the grandchildren. Every night he led them in prayers and hymn singing. He requested membership in the Presbyterian Church, keeping the promise he had made to his wife many years before. Some historians tell this story about the ceremony. One requirement for membership in the church was to answer the question: Can you forgive all your enemies? Jackson answered: "My political enemies, I can freely forgive; but as for those who abused me when I was serving my country in the field . . . that is a different case." The minister told him that he could not join unless he could forgive all. After a pause, Jackson agreed to try.

His sight and hearing failed. Tremors slowed his ability to write legibly. Somehow he found the strength to attend a celebration honoring him on the twenty-fifth anniversary of the Battle of New Orleans. He tried to shake everyone's hand and to respond to the cheers of the crowd, but he could not. Seeing his feeble frame and the pain in his face, most of the crowd stood back at a respectful distance.

He tried to influence the 1840 national elections. Jackson found the strength to write letters and editorials supporting Van Buren over the Whig candidate, William Henry Harrison. After telling audiences how to vote, he said, "Go to the polls like independent voters...and snatch the republican system from certain defeat...." When Harrison won, Jackson declared that corruption and bribery would now spread throughout the country. About a month after he took office, Harrison died suddenly of pneumonia. Jackson was delighted. He said, "The Lord ruleth, let our nation rejoice."

In the spring of 1842, his health declined again. His eyesight grew worse, and the constant pain in his head increased. In September 1842, he made out a new will. He asked that all his debts be paid out of his estate and that he be buried next to Rachel. He left the Hermitage to Andrew Jr.

When Texas was admitted to the union in 1845, the news cheered Jackson. Democrat James Polk, a native of Tennessee, was elected president in 1844, and Jackson replied, "I thank my god that the Republic is safe." Now he had to be propped up in bed when he wanted to read or write. The hemorrhaging continued, and his body swelled. "I am a blubber of water," he said. "How far my god may think proper to bear me up under my weight of afflictions, he only knows." He no longer had enough energy or breath to visit Rachel's grave.

Jackson asked that his grandchildren pay him a visit. He kissed and blessed each one, and he spoke with a strong voice about his faith in the Christian religion. "Do not cry—be good children and we will all meet in heaven." He told his family that he wanted to be buried without ostentatious display and with as little expense as possible.

Seventy-eight-year-old Andrew Jackson died on June 8, 1845. The funeral service, held at the Hermitage, was open to the public who were invited with a simple notice. Over 3000 mourners attended the service. In virtually every community in the country, flags flew at half-mast, papers were bordered in black, salute guns were heard. His body was laid to rest in the Hermitage garden beside his beloved Rachel.

Legacy

Jackson faced four major controversial issues during his career. In each of the four, he made up his mind about the best course of action, and he did not waver.

Removal of Native Americans: Jackson believed that removal was the act of a kindly father toward his dependent children. It was not. It was cruel and inhuman treatment. The forced removal of American Indians from their native lands is a disgraceful chapter in American history.

Nullification: Southern states used the term nullification to mean that they could declare any federal law null and void. They believed that the federal government would have to accept this action or to accept secession. Jackson held the view that no state could secede or nullify any federal law. To Jackson, an act of nullification was an act of treason. Arguments over states' rights versus federal responsibilities continue today.

Executive power: Jackson said the executive branch was more powerful than the legislative branch because the president was elected by all of the people while Representatives were elected by small groups of people.

Democracy: Jackson insisted that the president was the servant of the people. His broad definition of "the people" included the great masses of workers and farmers not just the rising businessmen and entrepreneurs. He urged citizens to express their opinions and, of course, to vote.

Andrew Jackson scored many firsts as president. He was the first person from the frontier to become the highest officer in the land. He was the first president to tell citizens that the government belonged to them. He was the first chief executive to tell Congress that it was he, not they, who held the ultimate power in the country. He was the first president to be censured. Jackson vetoed more bills than all his predecessors combined. He was the only president to pay off the national debt. The Age of Jackson remembered as the first organized attempt to reform government. Andrew Jackson reshaped American democracy with his doctrine that "The people are sovereign."

Appendix

The Five Civilized Tribes

Thousands of Native Americans were killed and thousands were exiled to the wilderness of the West because most white Americans believed that they could not become "civilized." A small number of Native Americans who evaded removal decided to become more like whites in order to avoid the punishment inflicted on other Indians. They created societies, modeled after those of the white men. They organized representative governing bodies, set up constitutions, established public schools, and were active in farming, trading, and other businesses. Many became Christians.

By the late eighteenth and early nineteenth centuries, white people were forced to reconsider their condemnation of all Native Americans as uncivilized. Could they condemn tribes modeled on their own communities? They could not. So they coined the phrase "Five Civilized Tribes" to indicate the tribes which were most like their own communities. Members of the Choctaw, Chickasaw, Seminole, Creek, and Cherokee comprised these tribes.

Choctaws: Members of this tribe originally lived in Georgia, Alabama, Mississippi, and Louisiana.

Chickasaws: Members of this tribe formerly lived in parts of what is now Mississippi, Tennessee, Kentucky, and Alabama.

Seminoles: The Seminole tribes developed in the nineteenth century from Creeks who settled in Spanish Florida.

Creeks: In the eighteenth century, the Creeks occupied most of what is now Alabama and Georgia.

Cherokees: In the early 1800s, the Cherokees lived in what is now North and South Carolina, Tennessee, Georgia, and Alabama.

Timeline

1767—Born in South Carolina on March 15.

1780-81—Serves in American Revolutionary War.

1787—Obtains license to practice law.

1791—Marries Rachel Donelson Robards.

1796—Elected to U. S. House of Representatives.

1797—Elected to U. S. Senate.

1802—Becomes major general of Tennessee militia.

1814—Commissioned major general in U. S. Army.

1814—Imposes martial law in New Orleans.

1818—Invades Spanish Florida.

1819—Faces Congressional censure.

1821—Becomes governor of Florida.

1825—Defeated for U. S. president in House election.

1828—Elected president of the U. S.

1828—Rachel dies of heart attack.

1830—Signs Indian Removal bill.

1832—Reelected President.

1836—Leaves Washington as ex-president.

1845—Dies at Hermitage.

Bibliography

Cole, Donald B. *The Presidency of Andrew Jackson.* Kansas: University Press, 1993.

Davis, Burke. *Old Hickory.* New York: The Dial Press, 1977.

Life Portrait of Andrew Jackson. Video. C-SPAN Archives. Indiana, 1999.

Marszalek, John. *The Petticoat Affair.* New York: The Free Press, 1997.

Peterson, Merrill D. *Olive Branch and Sword–The Compromise of 1833.* Baton Rouge: Louisiana State University Press, 1982.

Remini, Robert. *Andrew Jackson and the Course of the American Empire, 1767-1821.* New York: Harper & Row, Publishers, 1977.

―――. *Andrew Jackson and the Course of American Freedom, 1822-1832,* Vol. II. New York: Harper & Row, Publishers, 1981.

―――. *Andrew Jackson and the Course of American Democracy 1833-1845*, Vol. III. New York; Harper & Row, Publishers, 1984.

Schlesinger, Jr., Arthur. *The Age of Jackson.* Boston: Little, Brown and Company, 1945.

Watson, Harry L. *Liberty and Power.* New York: Farrar, Straus and Giroux, 1990.

Sources

CHAPTER ONE

p.10 "A memorandum..." Remini, Robert. *Andrew Jackson and the Course of the American Empire*. (Vol. I) New York: Harper & Row, Publishers, 1977, p.91.

p.12 "I was a skeleton..." Remini, op.cit., p.6.

p.14 "My character you have injured" Davis, Burke. *Old Hickory*. New York: The Dial Press, 1977, p. 14

p.15 "I fear that their Peace Talks..." Remini, op.cit., p.71.

p.18 "It has a flavor..." Remini, op.cit., p.26.

p.18 "been Grasping after power..." Remini, op.cit., p.94.

p.18 "My heart rests with you" Remini, op.cit., p.91.

CHAPTER TWO

p.19 "the opprobrium that has been attacked..." Davis, op.cit., p.108

p.22 "I shall expect..." Remini, op.cit., p.121.

p.23 "your conduct and expressions..." Remini, op.cit., p.140.

p.24 "less than two million..." Remini. op.cit., p.149.

p.26 "My pride is that my soldiers..." Remini, op.cit., p.160.

p.27 "As a military man..." Davis, op.cit., p.164.

CHAPTER THREE

p.29 "at a period like the present..."Remini, op.cit., p.171

p.29 "Do not, my beloved husband..." Remini. op.cit., p.173

p.30 "My blessed Redeemer..." Remini, op.cit., p.174.

p.30 "hypocritical Political Villains..."Remini, op.cit., p.176.

p.32 "Long will their General live..." Remini, op.cit., p.181.

p.32 "I'll keep my arm" Davis, op.cit., p.75.

p.33 "The Great Spirit gave..." Davis, op.cit., p.76.

p.33 "Let the white race perish!" Remini, op.cit., p.189.

p.34 "We must not await..." Remini, op.cit., p.190.

p.37 "I felt the pangs..." Remini, op.cit., p.201.

p.37 "You have only to act..." Remini. op.cit., p.204.

p.38 "The gratitude of a country..." Davis, op.cit., p.155.

p.40 "I am in your power..." Remini, op.cit., p.218.

p.40 "The bravery you have displayed..." Remini, op.cit., p.221.

p.24 "An Eye for an Eye..." Remini, op.cit., p.233.

CHAPTER FOUR

p.43 "If my demands are rejected..." Remini, op.cit., p.241.

p.43 "complexion was sallow..."Remini, op.cit., p.249.

p.44 "Be pleased to keep to yourself..." Remini, op.cit., p.254.

p.46 "By the Eternal..." Remini, op.cit., p.263.

p.46 "Don't mind the rockets..." Remini, op.cit., p.270.

p.47 "This supiness, this negligence..." Remini, op.cit., p. 273.

p.48 "How then could brave men..." Remini, op.cit., p. 287.

p.48 "Hail to the chief..." Remini, op.cit., p.291

p.50 "We are compelled therefore..." Davis, op.cit., p.56.

CHAPTER FIVE

p.51 "Brothers, Listen." Remini, op.cit., p.323.

p.52 "I conclude that Congress..." Remini, op.cit., p.326.

p.52 "Friends & Brethren..." Remini, op.cit., p.328.
p.56 "I am at present..." Remini, op.cit., p.364.

CHAPTER SIX
p.60 "a country of tall trees ..." Remini, op.cit., p.394.
p.61 "If you refuse..." Remini, op.cit., p.395.
p.62 "Oh, the wickedness..." Davis, op.cit., p.176
p.66 "do they think..." Davis, op.cit., p.182.
p.66 "I give the same answer..." Davis, op.cit., p.187.
p.67 "I hope he may not be called..." Davis, op.cit., p.183.
p.70 "Was there ever witnessed..." Remini, Robert. *Andrew Jackson and the Course of American Freedom* (Vol. II) New York: Harper & Row, Publishers, 1981, p.98.

CHAPTER SEVEN
p.74 "To the Polls" Remini (Vol II), op.cit., p.145.
p.74 "I had rather be..." Marszalek, John. *The Petticoat Affair.* New York: The Free Press, 1997, p.18.
p.75 "My heart is nearly broke." Marszalek, op. cit., p. 45.
p.78 "The mob broke in..." Remini (vol II) op.cit., p.17-18.
p.78 "Ladies fainted..." Marszalek, op.cit., p.72.
p.80 "female virtue is like..." Marszalek, op.cit., p.82.
p.82 "I was elected to pay..." Davis, op.cit., p.275.
p.83 "Our Federal Union" Watson, Harry. *Liberty & Power.* New York: Farrar, Straus and Giroux, 1990, p.96.
p.84 "South Carolina is oppressed..." Davis, op.cit., p.320.
p.84 "If this thing [secession]..." Remini Robert. *Andrew Jackson and the Course of American Democracy (Vol III)* p.16.
p.84 "The hope of the country..." Peterson, Merrill D. *Olive Branch and Sword—The Compromise of 1833* . Baton Rouge: Louisiana State University Press, 1982, p.39.

CHAPTER EIGHT

p.85 "To these laws . . ." Remini (Vol II), op.cit., p.269.

p.85 "God bless you . . ." Remini (Vol II), op.cit., p.271.

p.86 "the most profound hypocrite . . ." Remini (Vol III), op.cit., p.247.

p.87 "I only wish . . ." Marszalek, op.cit., p.180.

p.88 "The bank . . . is trying . . ." Davis, op.cit., p.305.

CHAPTER NINE

p.94 "a barbarian who could not . . ." Davis, op.cit., p.336

p.95 "Go to Nicholas Biddle . . ." Schlesinger, Jr., Arthur. *The Age of Jackson*. Boston: Little, Brown and Company, 1945, p.109.

p.95 "Though we live under . . ." Davis, op.cit., p.336.

p.95 "I look upon Jackson . . ." Schlesinger, Jr., op.cit., p.110.

p.95 "My own course is decided . . ." Schlesinger, Jr., op.cit., p. 102.

p.96 "We are in the midst . . ." Remini (Vol III), op.cit., p.125.

p.98 "The majority is to govern . . ." Remini (Vol III)., op.cit., p. 136.

p.102 "The cursed negroes were all . . ." Remini (vol III), op.cit., p.185.

p.104 "You have no right . . ." Remini (vol III), op.cit., p.306.

CHAPTER TEN

p.106 "The long sword of France . . ." Davis, op.cit., p.350.

p.108 "I have great confidence . . ." Remini (vol III), op.cit., p.273.

p.109 "if they touch the hair . . ." Remini (vol III), op.cit.,p.368.

p.110 "My own race is nearly run . . ." Davis, op.cit., p.362.

p.110 "Gentlemen, I am no longer President . . ." Remini, (vol III), op.cit., p.419.

p.112 "My political enemies . . ." Remini (Vol III), op.cit., p.446.

p.112 "Go to the polls . . ." Remini (vol III), op.cit., p.469.

p.113 "The Lord ruleth . . ." Remini (Vol III), op.cit., p.472.

p.113 "I thank my god . . ." Remini, (vol III) op.cit., p.508.

p.113 "I am a blubber . . ." Remini (Vol III), op.cit., p.519.

p.113 "do not cry . . ." *Life Portrait of Andrew Jackson.* C-span Videotape 122792, 1999.

Index